*Inspiring and transforming want to share it with many. Will keep reading for a very long time.

Rev Joy Shikmut - J.B. Shikmut Ministries

*This is a powerful and encouraging truth from a deep revelation and relationship with The Father. I know that these poems will bless all those who read and receive the truth set forth on these pages. Study it, embrace it and be blessed. Great work, Great truth for the weary soul. May all the readers of these truths find joy.

Bishop Dr. Emmanuel MacJones - God Pleasers Family International Church. Maryland

Dearly Beloved – "Apple of God's Eye" Is an excellent, masterful work which strongly reminds us of many truths presented in life's journey.

This book will ignite its readers mind to explore the deep reflections that are conveyed on the pages.

June Bainbridge - Retired Teacher - Maryland

Dearly Beloved – Apple of God's Eye." Encouraging words that bring healing and divine perspective for everyone who desires to reach his full potential as God's child.

Pastor Michael Wayne Wilson - One International Church, Maryland

Dearly Beloved "Apple of God's eye is a compilation of poetic creativity that reach through continuum of time to share a simple message. The call is for all persons to embrace the fullness of God's love and lavishly cherish and share it.

Rev Dr. Stacey Cole –Wilson - Executive Minister of Justice United Methodist Church, Baltimore Maryland.

ISBN 978-1-64458-977-9 (paperback)
ISBN 978-1-64492-046-6 (hardcover)
ISBN 978-1-64458-978-6 (digital)

Christian Faith Publishing, Inc.
832 Park Avenue
Meadville, PA 16335
www.christianfaithpublishing.com

Printed in the United States of America

DEARLY BELOVED—

Apple of God's Eye

Beverley Bennett

Contents

Acknowledgement

All my sisters, particularly Joy, Dawn, and Carol.

My friends: Valda, Joyce, Etta, Brudy, Ed, Shawna, Grace, Jean, Ilene, Damson and Isha, Pamry, Annette, Carmen, Mitchell, Sheron, June and her husband, Phyllis, Norman and Sonia, Josephine, Ruthven and Jackie, Retha, Leleith, Vera, Auldyth, Patrick, Fern, Pauline, Grace, Marlene, Kenrick, Charlotte, Gloria, Wayne, Stacey, Audrey and the many others who have not been mentioned.

Thanks for your love, encouragement, prayers and the contributions in making this effort possible.

Introduction

Dearly Beloved, Apple of God's Eye,

I would not have you to be uninformed or ignorant concerning the true nature and purpose of this book, but rather present to you a sincere, passionate, and clear account of a collection of messages written in regular form, prose, and poetic style and flavor proclaiming and emphasizing scriptural messages and revelation.

These messages are written with every human in
mind and are intended to alert, promote, and foster man's
need for a relationship with God.

This book is to:
The broken hearted;
The neglected and the molested;
The rejected and the wounded;
The joyful and the disheartened;
The husband and the wife;
The parent, the child, and the orphan;
The young and the old;
The male and female; and
The saved and the unsaved.

Without any reservation, the messages are meant
to be relevant and provide spiritual awareness to
the time in which we are living.
It is my greatest hope that it will provide you
with information that will
connect you to the truth of God's word.
For, indeed, I write in accordance and in obedience to the
script God has shared and downloaded to me.

I am, therefore, optimistic that it will build your
confidence and faith, encourage, empower, inspire,
and bring you joy and sweet peace, as you face life
and its challenges. I sincerely hope that
as you read you will be blessed
and that none will be lost.

And finally, Dearly Beloved,
God wants me to remind you that you are indeed
The Apple of His eye.

To You with Love

Dearly beloved,
Here is an invitation that is being extended to you with love.
Hope you'll take the time to read it through,
so that you can find out what next to do.
For it's not by chance that you have picked up this book
and it's not by chance that in it you look.
Each step of the way, I was directed and have committed to
put in writing and on display this message
designed for you this day.

So here is your chance to read and find out
what God has in his heart and desires for you to do.
Read it through carefully, read it
with enthusiasm, read it well.
And be prepared to share what you have read.
Do not hesitate to make it known.
Do it boldly.
Do it purposefully.
Do it wisely, promptly, honestly,
and without compromise.

You are *The Apple of God's eye* and that's so true.
I sincerely hope you will walk closely
with Him in all you do.
Seize the opportunity and seize it now,
Grasp the knowledge in it that you find.
Take hold of it and don't let it go.
Own it, work on it, live by it, and do not quit.
Be inspired, be encouraged, be entertained,
And you'll find out you've not read this book in vain.

For in these messages there's food to obtain
And wisdom you can't afford to abstain.

So be nurtured, my friend,
As you are richly fed.
May you experience supernatural strength, wealth, and health.
Be transformed within your heart, soul,
mind, body, and head.
And if you are down, quickly pick yourself up,
Brush off the dust, and make a fresh start.

A Change Is Coming

A change is coming my way and I believe it.
A blessing is coming my way and I receive it.
I hear the sound of abundance of rain.
Every valley shall be exalted.
Every mountain and hill made low.
The crooked made straight.
And the rough places made smooth.

The blessings of the Lord is overtaking me.
This is my season.
This is my new day.
I will rejoice in it,
for the mouth of the Lord has spoken it
And I believe it.
A change is coming my way,
thank God for it.

A Confused Generation

I gazed from my window, I saw them out in the street.
They were half naked and barefooted with maybe nothing to eat.
I ran down the stairs to take a closer peep
and, oh, what I saw I began to weep.

They were stained with dirt up to the teeth.
And their skins looked out from almost head to feet.
What they were wearing was more than skin deep.

I walked out my doors to follow them up the street
to see where they were heading, as I silently weep.
I could smell trouble as they quickly moved their feet.
They wanted attention, they wanted everybody to know,
they were the needy and hurting people lost in the street.

They are the neglected and they are the runaways.
They are teenagers, they are our neighbors
but, most importantly, they are human.
"Oh God," I said. "Please help them to find some help."
They stomped their feet, hurled threats, yelled
and screamed at the top of their voices,
and blamed everyone but themselves for setbacks and defeats.

It was obvious that they were angry and confused.
It was obvious that too much had been going on
and they have missed the right way.
So, Lord, grant us the strategy and show us the way
to reach this generation who have lost their way.

A Day to Laugh

Let today be that day filled with laughter.
A day filled with peace, joy, and love,
forgetting all the bad times you've had.
The days of disappointments, pain, and sufferings,
let them not be remembered anymore.

Today is that day of new beginnings.
A day of discovery, a day to celebrate.
A day of amazing transformation.
A day to embrace, rejoice, and be glad.
A day to laugh in the devil's face.
A day to reminisce on the greatness of God.

Begin today with positive emotion.
Smile, laugh, and feel good.
Wake up the best in you,
Provoke it into action.
Let it spread all over you.
Let it be memorable, let it be sweet.
Put away the unwholesome, ugly
memories of yesterday.
Let them not haunt, deter, or get in your way.

Let today come forth, draped in beauty and energy.
Let today be the day to laugh, feel healthy and good.
Let everything that hath breath give praises for
a day such as this.
Let laughter come easily.
Let today be for you a refreshing, fruitful,
and unforgettable day.

Add Something Good and Wonderful

Add a little sunshine to brighten up your life.
Add a little spice to make things sweet and nice.
Add some fragrance to keep foul smell at bay.
Make your life beautiful by always
adding something good and wonderful.

Make life worthwhile, if you have to live it.
Make your life a storybook and let others enjoy reading it.
Always add something that is powerful.
Make your life a modeled life that
others would like to live.
Make your life good and wonderful by
keeping God in it.

After the Storm

It's time to pick up the pieces.
It's time to calculate the damage.
It's time to reflect on the providence of God.
It's the time to praise and thank Him.

The storm has finally passed.
What a night it has been!
The hands of death came pretty close
but did not triumph over me.
The feet of death passed by,
but it did not trample or overcome me.
Thank God the worst has passed.

After the storm, the dark clouds have vanished.
After the storm, there is peace.
After the storm, it's time to reflect on God's mercy.
After the storm, there comes a calm.

All Things Are Possible with God

There's no problem that God cannot solve.
No mountain that He cannot move.
No ocean too wide that He will not allow you to cross,
If only you allow Him to be the boss.

Nothing is impossible with the Almighty God,
Not even that which is impossible with man.
He has the amazing ability to turn around storms.
The supernatural and awesome power to call forth a calm.

There's nothing that He cannot undo,
Nothing that the devil may have thrown at you.
He's a God of miracles, working wonders
by the minute and the hour.
There's nothing impossible with Him,
Not even that which you think He can't do.

There's nothing that God cannot do.
With Him, it's not maybe or perhaps in anything.
If He says it, He will surely prove it.
If He approves it, He can bring it, and if He brings it,
He can remove it.

He helped the Israelites to cross over the Red Sea.
He helped them to cross over the Jordan
and to break down the Jericho walls.
There's absolutely nothing that He cannot do,
Not even that which seems impossible with you.

All Is Not Lost

If you've suffered disappointment, you are not alone.
If you've suffered loss, others have been there, too.
If you've loved and lost, think not of yourself as the only one.
If you've been lied to, there are many others who
have borne that heavy cross, too.
If you've tried and failed, you are not alone for there
are many others who have been in your shoes.
If you've been knocked down and out, you
can live to rise again.
All is not lost.

All is not lost, even though you are down and it may seem so hard.
All is not lost, even when you've fallen underground.
All is not lost, even though many may have told you so.
All is not lost, no matter how it feels or looks.
All is not lost until one is physically and spiritually dead.
All is not lost until one is eternally separated from God.

An Enemy Came in to Rob Me (Testimony)

He left his place of abode and sneaked into my room.
I woke up in the middle of the night and felt
his hands holding me tight.
He blurred my vision, then aimed his attacks at
my head, throat, and heart.
He tortured me throughout the rest of the night,
then disappeared
when it was morning light.

I thought it would have been his only visit
but I was wrong, for then he came back
again and again.
It took me a while but, eventually, I learnt his name
and his evil intentions.

Of course, he immediately wanted me to believe my
friends and family had abandon me. Of course,
he wanted me to be sorry for myself,
So he aimed at bullying me into believing his lies.
He wanted me to believe he was on my side
and he came by to rescue me.
He told me the biggest lies I might have
ever heard in my life.

As you may imagine, it was not an easy fight.
He persisted and I resisted.
I battled with him day and night.
I read my Bible, fasted, and prayed,
but this lying, uninvited, unwelcome visitor only
harassed me again and again.

You wouldn't believe the pain he caused.
You wouldn't believe the struggles I had.
But I remain determined that he would not have my mind,
and that I would live and would not die.
He, too, was determined and would not quit,
and I would not give up or give into his torture and tricks.
The battle was hot and very fierce and raged on many
nights, but God, in His mercy, protected my mind.

You may not understand because you have never been there.
You may never imagine what's it's like when the enemy
wants to take over your mind and by this you might
have guessed his name.
He's called Depression and he has no shame.

I am proud to make this report and tell you that
I have not lost my mind.
I am more alert than at any other time in my life.
I am victorious.
I am determined.
I am a fighter indeed.
I am a winner.
I am more than a conqueror with God
working on my side.

Anxieties

Take control of your anxieties
or they will take control of you.
Be anxious for nothing,
But in everything, give thanks.
Be diligent, steadfast, and true,
Letting not your anxiety lord over you.

Say to anxieties, "I will not entertain you.
I will not allow you to rule over me.
For in the name of Jesus, I say goodbye to you."
Don't be overwhelmed.
Take life easy and right.
Don't be anxious about anything.
God is always on time.

Aren't You Glad?

Aren't you glad that God is on your side?
Aren't you glad that He is your final authority?
Aren't you glad that He's just, faithful, and kind?
Aren't you glad that He makes no mistake
in judging us?
Aren't you glad?

Aren't you glad that God is master, author,
and finisher of our faith?
Aren't you glad that it's up to Him to
determine our next move?
Aren't you glad that He never fails and
He never backs down?
Aren't you glad that human destiny and outcome
are part of His plan?
Aren't you glad?

In God's sight, all are considered equal. Aren't you glad?
Think about what it would be like if your life
was all left up to man.
Aren't you glad that no matter how things look
or feel, they are subject to His will and control?
Aren't you glad?
You should be exceedingly glad.

Are You a Friend of God?

If not a friend, then you are an enemy.
There is no middle ground.
It's either-or.
If you are not for Him, you are against Him.
Where do you stand?
Ask yourself now:
Who or what are you for?

You can't serve two masters.
You'll love one and hate the other.
Great smiles and good deeds will not be enough.
They guarantee you no place in the kingdom.
You must have a heart built on God's word.
Ask yourself if you are being a friend or a foe.
Of course, you ought to know.

Are you a friend of God, trusting in His word?
Do you know Him as you ought to know?
No friend is greater having than Him.
Nothing is sweeter than living for Him.
Are you being a friend to Him?
Nothing in this life can be better than serving Him.

Are You Faced with a Mountain?

Is there a mountain in your way?
Speak to it right now,
Tell it to go away.
Speak to it with confidence.
Be fearless, speak out, and do not doubt.
You have the information and authority
to speak to mountains and bring them down.

To speak to your mountain, no one has to help you out.
No one has to come to your rescue.
No one has to fly in from out of town.
No one can speak to your mountain like you.
Speak to it, let it crumble, and disappear from you.
All you have to do is release your faith
and use the word of God to knock it down.

The enemy knows when you are blocked in.
The enemy recognizes when you have doubts.
The enemy knows what it is to have a mountain
standing in your way.
What the enemy might not know is that
you have a powerful word in your mouth
that can bring him and your mountain to the ground.

So speak to your mountain now.
Open wide your mouth and let the word out.
Tell your mountain what the word is all about.
Speak to your mountain, speak and never doubt.
Speak to your mountain, it will surely crumble
and fall down.

Are You That Person God Is Looking For?

God is looking for people who will willingly worship and adore Him.
He's looking for people who will zealously seek after Him.
He's looking for a people that require all of Him.
He's looking for people who will hunger and thirst after Him.
He's looking for people that will go all the way with Him.
Are you that person that God is looking for?

He is not looking for the righteous but for sinners to come after Him.
He's not looking for coldness, neither for the lukewarm.
He's looking for people that require the fire of God within.
He's not looking for a people whose desire is to be ruled by sin.
He's not looking for people attached to fame, name, and buildings.
He's looking for a people unattached to anything but Him.
He's looking for people who will honor Him.

He's not looking for eloquent speakers, teachers, or preachers.
But He's looking for anointed, devoted servants who
will uncompromisingly divide His word.
He's not looking for entertainers, shouters, or dancers.
He is not looking for so-called prophets,
so-called tongue talkers, or make-belief interpreters.
He is looking for people who will courageously speak
the words from Him.

God is looking for Bible-believing truth revealers who
will speak as the Spirit leads them, people who
will proclaim the gospel truth of God.
He is looking for real people, a people that will
hunger and thirst for everything from Him.
He's looking for people who desire to live and reign with Him.
Is that you?

Arise, My Beloved

Arise, it is day.
Arise and wipe your tears away.
Arise and come away from the dust
and the heat.
Arise and robe yourself right
and be ready for the task, be ready for the fight.

Look around you,
God is making room for you.
He's opening doors and windows, too.
Arise, my beloved, to a brand–new
and beautiful day.
Arise, my beloved,
there's work for you to do.
Rise to that place that God has called you.

Rise like the sun,
Like the eagle,
Like the charming, peaceful dove.
Arise and come forth,
Bring forth that radiance,
that fragrance within you.
Arise, my beloved,
There are people waiting for you.

Back from the Dead

They sounded an alarm to say that he was dead.
They used a black cloth to cover his head.
No tears were shed.
No eulogy was read.
They told his few friends to go
quickly, bury their dead.

They complained that he stunk.
One could smell him from afar.
They made comments.
They rehearsed his failures and all.
He could not see the ugly faces they made.
He said nothing.
He just laid there.
He was dead.

But when a voice from out of nowhere
uttered his name
And told him to get up, live, walk,
and run again.
He rose up quickly,
shook himself, and began his journey
in Jesus's name.
Now he shares his story. He named it,
Back from the Dead.

Behold, I Live Again

Up from the grave I came
After being dead for years, months,
and many days.
After being eulogized and thrown in a grave
for sins committed and uncommitted.
Buried deep and covered from head to toe
With a sign affixed upon my grave
That read, "Executed for Sin and Shame."

Oh, my God, my body sunk beneath
the added weight.
And I must have stunk so much that even
the worms and flies complain.
So battered and wounded in life, I could
not live another day.
So dead, I was, and now so deeply buried.
No amount of human pulling could bring
me up from where I was.
Nobody cared to have me around,
I was considered useless
and unwanted baggage. After all, that's
what some people claim.

But in life I did cry out to the one above.
In pain I asked for help.
But to live I had to die, and when death came,
It took God Himself to resurrect me to life again.
He remembered me.
He had compassion on me.
He rolled away the stones from the entrance to my grave.
He unbounded me from my guilt, pain, and shame.
And now I am alive and well again with a testimony to give.

Be Not Afraid

Be not afraid, God is with you.
He has not forsaken or forgotten you.
Be not afraid, but
Be bold,
Be brave,
Be steadfast and confident, always trusting in God.

"Fear not" is what the Bible says.
Fear not, for fear is not of God,
So be not afraid.
You cannot win the battle being afraid
or being a coward.
Look the adversary squarely in the face
and let him know that you are not afraid.
Take a page out of David's book
and do not allow the enemy to scare
you with his words or looks.

Be not afraid,
But be strong and never doubt.
Let God be the strength of your life.
Always consider yourself a champion for Him,
He is on your side.
Expect to be the winner each time you fight,
For He's more than able to deliver you
in the time of trouble.

Be not afraid to bind the strong man.
Always call upon God to help you out.
Be not afraid, for with God there's no doubt that
He'll find a way to bring you out.

Be Not Ashamed

There is something extraordinary about Jesus,
Something marvelous about Him and His name.
If you happen to experience or have an encounter with Him,
You'll find out you'll never be the same.

You will never be ashamed of His record,
His birth, life, works, or death.
And when it comes to His resurrection, it's
the best story yet.

Though some may complain and criticize
your association with Him,
Be not ashamed.
Be not ashamed to say that you know Him.
Be not ashamed to say that you are one of His.
Tell of your marvelous encounter with Him.
Tell how He called you out of darkness, placed
you in His glorious light.
Tell how He saved your soul from sin.
Be not ashamed.

Be not ashamed to show your affection for Him.
Boast like St. Paul and be not ashamed.
Be not ashamed to grasp any opportunity
to speak out about Him.
Be not ashamed.
Take a stand for Him and be not ashamed.

Be Your Brother's Keeper

Be your brother's keeper,
Stop shaking him down.
Stop shoving him under the bus.
Stop selling him out to others.
Stop stabbing him in the back.

If you see him in shark-infested water,
Why not try to get him out, clean up his wound,
and get him back on good and solid ground?
If he has fallen down, why not pick him up and
try to get him back on track?
Remember, he is your brother.

Let it not be in you to keep a brother down.
Remember, you are his keeper, believe it or not.
You should not be shouting triumph when
he has fallen down.
You don't have to read him the riot act and
call the army out.
Neither do you have to read his eulogy
nor preach to him his death sermon before he's dead.
He's your brother,
don't try to keep him down.

Be your brother's keeper and try to keep him around.
Don't keep him down.
Be your brother's keeper. Try to keep him alive, active, and well.
You don't have to give him the death sentence and cheer him on
into hell.
Instead, help him to live and find peace in God.
Show him that you really care and want to love and honor him.
Be your brother's keeper and help to keep him out of sin and hell.

38

Blocked In

Aren't there times in life when it seems you are blocked in, fenced in,
and completely surrounded by the enemy and his wimps?
But do you realize that the enemy's plan is to keep
you in doubt, trapped, and blocked in?
Satan's job is to create confusion.
His job is to create doubts.
He will try to keep you bound.
He will try to keep you blocked in.

In this life, you will encounter roadblocks
and stumbling blocks, too.
But do not let any of the devil's blocks become your full stop.
For though there are walls intended to keep you from
looking or getting out, it takes a shout-out to God to
get you over and out.
A mighty shout when applied will surely cause the walls
to come tumbling down.

When it seems that you are blocked in
And you think there's no way out,
do not be afraid.
Your way of escape is already made.
At the right time, God will lead you to it.
The enemy will not win, his strategies are unwise,
So waste not your time worrying.
Without a doubt, God will surely get you out.

Blocked, Stopped, Trapped

You woke up, it's the middle of the night.
You are feeling trapped, bombarded on every side.
You are locked in and fenced in from outside in.
The walls around you seemed too hard to climb
And the skies above you reveal hardly any light
But surely seemed to indicate there will be trouble tonight.

You cannot run and you cannot hide.
Your feet is fixed and your hands are tied.
You are trapped on every side, it seemed.
But life, as you know, must go on.
"Face it or be sure to die!" you seemed to hear it screamed.
Do not complain or try to negotiate, this is your fate.
Accept it.

You pushed back the covers.
You wipe the perspiration from your face.
You begin to think you don't know for how long you did,
Then out of the stillness of the night
There seemed to appear someone as if by your side.
You looked around, then heard a voice whispering in your ears,
"I have a solution for you, my child.
Choose life, do not give in.
Do not fall into despair.
All is not lost, I am here. Behold, I care."

This is the middle of the night
and you know you are not dreaming or losing your mind,
so up from bed you quickly get
and now you must try to think and relax.
Clear as crystal and sure as day, it's affirmed that
to escape and to survive, you must depend on Jesus Christ.

For true relief and for peace of mind,
One must call upon God every day.
To remove the trap and see your way,
You must resort to the godly map—the Bible.
And that's the only way to prevent being
blocked, stopped, or trapped.

Blow the Whistle on the Devil

Blow the whistle on the devil,
Hold no secret for him.
Expose and disarm him,
Do not enable or befriend him.
Keep away from him.

Keep blowing the whistle on the devil.
Always work against him.
Have no conversation or dealing with him,
Only rebuke, discredit, and resist him.

Blow the whistle on the devil, wound him as often as you can.
Be strong, be diligent, be wise, and always be conscious of who he is.
He is cunning.
He is crafty.
He is deceptive.
He's after you to harm and destroy you,
But you can always outwit him using God's master plan.

Blow the whistle on the devil.
Never give place to him or ears to his enticing.
Do not accommodate, entertain, or trust him.
But always be willing, ready, and careful to show and tell the world
how best to defeat, disarm, or disable him.

Bring It On

Bring on the gospel, the good news of Jesus Christ,
and His love for mankind.
Let the people know they need Him in their lives.
Be not ashamed to make it known wherever man resides.

Don't be intimidated,
for if we must, live the abundant life,
then we must have Jesus Christ.
If we must embrace, let Him.
If we must lift up, let it be His name.
If we must stand, let's stand for loyalty to Him.
If we must look, let us look only to Him.
Bring it on.

Bring on the glorious Gospel of Jesus Christ.
Bring on the word, the word of life.
Bring on the truth.
Bring on the light.
Bring it on.
Bring it on if it embraces Jesus Christ.

Bring it on.
Bring on the glorious Gospel of Christ.
Let it be heard far, near, and wide.
Spread the good news wherever man is found.
Bring it on.
Bring it on now, the Gospel of Jesus Christ, love for mankind.

Broken and Deserted People

We see them every day.
Tired, haggard, hungry-looking faces,
Stained, jagged hands,
Toothless gums,
Dried, cracked lips, and tongue,
Smelly armpits,
Dry, scaly, cracking feet,
We see them here and there.
We see them hanging out on our streets
and in some of our villages and towns.

Some have lost their loved ones
And many have lost hope.
Some are deserted and have no place to go or to call home.
These are broken people.
These are people in need.
They are disheartened.
They are all trapped in despair and distress.

Broken and deserted people, yes, they are God's children, too.
He sees and hears everything they do and say,
Every word they utter, every tear they cry,
every insult they suffer, every shame and disappointment they face.
He never abandons, rejects, neglects, or forgets them.
And although you may not hear about it, witness it or understand
it.
He keeps them on His radar and in some supernatural way.
He provides and ministers to them every day.

Broken Days—Go to God

The days when you are feeling lonely,
feeling miserable, confused, and weary,
brokenhearted, drained, and worn out,
Go to God.

Go to God to fix it.
Go to Him for your happiness.
Find this place of comfort and safety,
go to Him for your relief.
Get out of your brokenness
and go to Him for assistance.
Go to Him for guidance and direction.

There'll be days of anxiety,
days of uncertainty and confusion,
but if you go to God, in Him you will
find love, joy, and peace of mind.
Go to Him with all your burdens.
Go to Him with your brokenness.
Go to Him for your every need you have.
He has the answers.
He offers solutions
to those who call out in distress.

But What Do You Say?

We say that we believe in God, yet we do not totally trust Him.
We say that His word is the final authority, yet we do not live by it.
We say that we honor His word, but when the Bible says
we all have sinned, we question and resent it.
We claim that we believe in Him but in fact we do not even know
Him.
We say that we'll follow Him but we always run ahead of Him
We say that He's our Lord and King, yet we worship
and pay homage to images and idols.
We say that we'll wait on Him, yet we show that
we have no time for Him.
We run ahead of Him, denounce and reject Him.
We say we love Him, yet we disrespect,
disobey, and dishonor Him.
What do you really say when it comes to Him?

Call It What It Is—Sin

Call it by its name.
Call it what it is.
Don't try to glamorize or colorize or popularize it.
Don't try to hide it.
Call it by its name.

It is what it is.
It will never change.
It's not to be glorified but to be defied.
Don't try to whitewash or sanitize it.
Call it its name and never be ashamed.

If God says it is sin, then why not call it that?
Why try to call it by some wholesome name?
Why try to paint, trivialize, or idolize it?
Why try to make it look good, feel good, or taste good?
Sin of any size, form, fashion, or shape remains sin.
It is presumptuous and abominable that what
God denounces and calls evil, we choose to call it good.

Do not try to suppress the truth about sin.
Don't try to entertain, favor, or sympathize with it.
Speak out against it.
Call it what it is.
Call it by its name.
Call it a sin if it is a sin.
You may be persecuted for speaking against it,
but you will never regret it.

Choose the Word of God

I went looking for a healthy lifestyle.
I looked here and there.
I could almost think I looked everywhere.
When I looked on the supermarket shelves,
I didn't find it there.
I looked to every farm product,
Neither was it there.

I looked to the doctors and nutritionists.
I tried everything they prescribed and described.
I followed through with all the exercises the gymnast
offered and presented.
But with all of what I did, it didn't provide the best result.
After a while of searching, I decided it was time
to give up and die.

I realized I really needed true help.
I got to the point where I became disillusioned
and got to the sad conclusion that my life was out of hand.
It was then someone introduced me to the Word of God.
He called it the word of life.
At first, I was skeptical I couldn't understand
how words printed in the Bible could help
me to a healthy lifestyle,
yet save my life.

It took some time, but I came to understand that the
words were not mere words printed on a page
but were supernatural, life-giving, and sustaining instructions.
I started out slowly to read the lines.
It soon became my daily and necessary bread—
a well-prepared and balanced meal and medication, too.

And now I know that to be in the best of health, one
must follow the Bible's instruction and take the full
dosage of the Word and in the amount the Lord prescribed.
Choose your words wisely. Choose the Word of God.

Come

Come with your burdens,
your fears, and your cares.
Come with your sorrows, pain, and tears.
Come lay them down at Jesus's feet.
Lay right there.

Come.
Come just as you are.
Come ready for a makeover
Come ready and prepared.
Come for a new life start.
Come, get to your feet, make the move.
Come now or then you may be too late.

Come.
Come now.
Come away from sin and sorrow.
Come, this may be your last and final call.
Come. Jesus says come.

Come Follow Him

Come follow Jesus.
He is going places.
He's meeting people.
He is changing lives.
Come follow Him.

See Him do some strange but
extraordinary things.
See Him converse with people,
supernaturally heal the sick, and raise the dead,
Meet with the poor, the rich, the religious,
and the political, too.
Provide, expose, rebuke, overturn,
or override some of their wills and plans.

Come follow Jesus,
accept His salvation.
Listen to some wonderful teachings,
experience His amazing power, identify
with Him.

Come follow Jesus.
Learn how to solve problems, increase your energy.
Learn the art of multiplication, attract crowds.
Come learn how He shares the truth.
Come follow Him.
Come follow Him now.
He will lead you away from sin.

Come Look for Me

Where the stars are,
where there's laughter,
where the grass is green,
the nightingale sings
and flowers bloom.
Where butterflies dance
and leaves flutter in the breeze.

Come look for me at the break of day
at the time the sun arises to welcome the day.
Come look for me in the church as
I whisper and pray.
Come look for me where there's love,
joy, peace, and liberty.

I will not linger where there's war and strife.
I will not hold on to misery, disappointments, and pain.
Don't look for me where there's fighting and backbiting.
I must be found among the hopeful and faithful.
I will be found among the blessed and the beautiful.
I will be with the wise and the wonderful.
That's where I belong.
I will be there to answer to my name.

Come look for me where there's music,
Where the ocean greets the land,
Where the mountains clap their hands,
Where the joyful sing their best songs,
Where the heaven reaches out to man.
Come look for me,
I will be in that place.

Come look for me
In a holy place.
Come look for me as I inquire
and aspire for the things of God.

Daniel and the Lions

The scripture says Daniel was a young man who was exiled in Babylon.
He purposed in his heart that from godly principles he would not
depart.
According to the book, he was not a coward.
He would not compromise.
For the truth of God, he would even chance his life.
He had an unwavering trust and would not violate his belief in God.
So he continued in his devotional habits, always praying and
praising God,
even when he landed in exile land.

In Babylon he was well favored.
He was skillful, wise in knowledge, and understanding.
However, when offered the King's provision,
he chose to make a godly decision.
He refused to eat of the king's meat and to drink of his wine
because that would be to his defeat and his demise.
Even when he knew his life was on the line
And even then, in this strange land, he would not compromise.

Yes, Babylon was a city of great wealth, influence, and power.
A place where cruelty and evil abound.
But Daniel remained steadfast and poised,
looking unto none other than his God.
He was not fainthearted.
He was consecrated and strong hearted.
He was not feeble nor wimpy but was bold, brave, and lion-hearted.
He firmly believed his God to be true, sincere, powerful, and wise.
He knew that his God would always be with him, acting on his side,
even while he was exiled in a heathen land.

The night before Daniel was expected to lose his life,
the palace folks could not sleep. They could not wait for the daylight.
From such cruel and wicked kind of drama,
they did not want to stay away.
They arose early that morning, maybe to witness
Daniel wrestle, wail, and beg for his life.
The lions were particularly made very hungry that day.
They were left unfed and prepared to charge at him
and tear him to pieces.
Oh yes, they were.

On this day as the gates were opened, there was
a moment of silence as the lions came charging
and roaring by with their cruel claws and wicked jaws.
They came bounding, leaping, and jumping
fiercely, savagely, and high.
The momentum build and the suspense grew,
as the crowd grew wild.
Many might have felt some coldness running
down their spine.
But when suddenly the lions dropped their paws,
stopped short to lick
and caress Daniel's hands, the hush was much.

None of the eyewitnesses could believe their eyes.
But Daniel remained cool, confident,
and calm throughout all this time
Because he knew that his loving God was on his side.
He knew that because of God's providence the lions'
mouths were shut.
The crowd couldn't believe what they saw.
They couldn't believe their eyes.
They were startled.
They were dumbstruck.

It must have been a remarkable and unbelievable sight,
as the onlookers must have shouted and some must
have even cried and prayed.
Some might have feared, while others jeered.
But whether they feared, cheered, or jeered,
when it was over, no manner of hurt on Daniel was found.

Daniel's God had preserved him from the lions' attack.
His life was spared because he dared to believe in his God.
His life was spared because he relied completely on the living God.
He did not allow himself to be scared and persuaded by man or
beast.
He did not give into worship of strange gods
even while exiled in a foreign, heathen, wicked, and cruel land.

Dare to Be Different

Dare to be different in all that you do.
Dare to be counted a doer of God's word.
Stand up for Jesus,
stand firm, faithful, and true.
Be bold and be diligent,
always observing His word.

Be steadfast and strong.
Hold fast to the right
and let go of the wrong.
Dare to be Christlike
in all that you do.
Let Christ be known wherever you go.
Speak with authority.
Speak with authenticity.
Speak God's word. Say it with all your might.

Call forth that which you have been waiting for.
Decree, declare, command, and demand
mountains and hills to tumble and fall,
kings and kingdoms to bow to Him now,
strongholds to be broken, and for
God to have His perfect way.

Dare to be different and dare to draw a line.
Dare to take a worthwhile and bold stand at all times.
Dare to live by your biblical principles,
practices, and codes.
Even if you have to stand alone,
dare not to compromise your conviction.

Give no place to the devil,
You are here to represent Jesus Christ.
Don't try to fit in with the world and its people.
Be not transformed by the world
but be transformed by the word of God.

Don't cave in.
Don't back down.
Don't substitute the truth for a lie.
Never move the standard to accommodate
misgivings and wrongs in order
to be perceived as loving, kind, and nice.
But always stand up for what's honorable
and true, good, and wise.
You could lose friends and family
when you stand for the right, but
dare to be different.
Dare to be strong.
Dare to be wise.
That's being Christlike.

Darkness Does Not Abide Here

Darkness does not live here,
Neither is it a friend of mine.
I asked it not to knock on my doors
or even come close to my property line.
God's light has been turned on in me
and I want to keep it burning bright.
I want to keep darkness away from me
and completely out of my life.
That would be my greatest delight.

I do not believe in darkness, I love and appreciate light.
I despise and reject the ways of darkness,
I embrace and adore true light.
I do not entertain darkness, it will not be a part of my life.
I welcome The Light.
I will gladly open my heart—the windows
and doors of my heart—to allow light to come in.
Darkness does not abide here, for Jesus is here to stay.

Jesus is The Light. He offers the opportunity
to see things bright.
Darkness signifies an evil omen that
tries to cover the light.
Darkness is an obstacle, a stumbling block to the right way.
It attracts trouble.
It may cause one to fall.
It is usually up to something foolish,
it's sometimes used as a trap.
It is a woeful enemy,
therefore it has no place with me.

Declare It

Let it be known throughout the four corners of this earth.
Let it be known to all humankind.
By your action and words, publicize it.
Make it known that Jesus Christ is Lord.
Declare it from the valley to the mountaintop
and the hills below.
Let those who have not known it hear
it loud and clear.
It is the truth, the living truth,
and all people ought to know it.

Declare it.
Jesus Christ is the life, the truth, and the only way.
Let it echo in your city and in your town.
Be persistent.
Be diligent
In letting it known.
There's none like Him.
There has been none before Him and neither
shall there be one after Him.
He came to give us life and it's for us to receive it,
therefore lift up your voice and
Declare it and pursue it.

Defy the Devil

Don't tell me I can't when God says I can.
Don't tell me I won't when God says I will.
Don't tell me it's never when God says it shall.
Don't tell me it will when God says it won't.
Devil, you are a liar.
I won't listen to your voice.
I will defy you.

I look to God to work for me.
I do not rely on self.
I do not entertain doubts and fears.
I chose to hug, kiss, embrace, and hang out with faith.
I do not take God's word for granted.
I feed on it.
It's my lifeline,
I boldly speak it
It has first place in my head, heart, soul, and life.

Divorce the Old Man

Divorce the old man,
He is not good for you.
Serve him notice, walk away from him, and do not look back.
Take a good look at yourself and see some of what he has done to you.
Divorce him now,
Get rid of him fast, or he will either seriously harm or kill you.

Divorce the old man,
Take on the new.
He is suitable and perfect for you.
Give back the old name, accept and claim the new.
Divorce the old man, he was not meant for you.

Years of abuse, rejection, and strange living.
Years of beatings, hunger, and strife.
Years of living in bondage and without Christ.
Divorce the old man, he's robbing you of a good life.
Seek out for help while there's time.
Take on the new man, the man Jesus Christ.

Don't Dare to Leave Home without Him

Don't dare to leave home without God.
Take Him everywhere you go.
You just don't know when you will need Him to represent you
or to be there to whisper a comforting word or two.
"Be still, my child, for lo, I am here with you."

You don't have to make appointments when you need to call on Him
To accompany you on your next trip to wherever you may have to go.
He will gladly make Himself available to share time with you.
After all, He is your Energizer Bunny, full of life
and will always work for you.
He is that type of person who will always want to be with you.

His company is always essential.
It's most vital to human lives,
for He keeps you out of trouble and keeps you well advised.
He appreciates when you show that His company is to your delight.
He is that friend and lover you should never leave behind or out of sight.
Never leave home without Him when you have to get on a flight.
Let Him buckle up beside you
or you could be in for the worst ride of your life.

Don't leave home without Him, for any business you have to do.
When next you have to go shopping, take him all the way with you.
Take Him to the restaurants, supermarkets, and the clothing store, too.
Don't leave home without Him is my advice to you.
Keep Him closer than your wallet, purse, credit or debit card,
keep him next to you.

If not, you could run into unexpected trouble—
ones too difficult for you to undo.

If you have to visit the doctor, make sure He goes with you.
Keep Him close to your heart, ears, and pocket,
for the cost and the diagnosis could certainly
overwhelm and scare you.
You can't afford to be without Him.
Keep him always as your life support and lifeline.

Don't leave home without Him.
Don't dare to take the chance.
Don't ever leave Him behind
or you could lose your life at any time.
Be focused, be very careful, too, for you just
don't know where, how,
or when you will run into sin.

Therefore, take no chance to ever leave Him behind,
not even for a short time.
Or you may get pounced on, get badly
harmed, or robbed of your life.
Don't leave home without Him is my advice to you.

Don't Fake It

Never you try to fake it, always be authentic,
For God knows all about it.
You may try to do it, believing you are fooling Him.
But get with it, you are only fooling yourself.
Never you try to fake it.
He knows when you are playing a part.

Man looks at the outward,
But God looks within.
He knows all the secrets.
He knows everything.
He knows you from the inside out.
He searches and knows the heart.
Don't try to fake it, He knows when you are acting.

If you are presenting a false image,
Before you start it, He knows about it.
And before long, your sin will be found out.
The Holy Spirit will surely convict you.
Your sinful action will bring shame on you.
You are no exception, therefore, try to do what's right.
Never try to fake it.
Faking it is deceptive and malicious,
and that's called sin.

Dry Bones Can Live Again

Dry bones in the valley, you can live again.
Though you seem dead,
There's life being offered to you.
Dry bones in the valley, hold up your head.
I prophesy to you.
I speak life over you.
I call you forth from the grave.
I say to you, "Dry bones, you can live again."

Can these dry live?
Yes, they can.
Dry bones will survive.
They will create a shaking.
They will put on flesh.
Blood will flow again.
They will come together in Jesus's name.

If you are a dry bone,
You can live again.
Hear the word of God,
Take a hold on it.
Speak change to your dryness.
Call forth power and life in it.

Evil Will Not Win

Evil will not win.
It will not prevail.
God is sovereign, always trust in Him.
Keep in His word.
He is in control.
He knows what He's doing.
Evil will not triumph, it will not win.
It will fail.

Don't go by what you see.
Evil will flourish but for a time.
It will not triumph over good.
It will come behind.
It will not win.
It will not prevail.
It will not be victorious over what is good and kind.

Although we wrestle not against flesh and blood,
God is in control.
So do not worry,
Evil will not triumph.
It will not prosper.
It will not stop the truth.
God will always have the last word and the final say,
And that's what will prevail.
Evil will not win.

From This Day Forward

I walk with God
From this day forward. I take a stand.
I commit myself to walk in victory.
Supernatural blessings are overtaking me.
I am convinced and fully confident that
God's Word is working for me.

From this day forward, I confess life has changed for me.
I gladly take my place among the blessed, the joyful, the
highly favored, the bold, and the free.
I sit in heavenly place. I am in line with the called out,
the selected. and the confirmed.
Thank God for this.
From this day forward, I declare my liberty.
I declare I have got the victory.

Get Out of the Valley, Get to the Mountaintop

You have seen the hopelessness,
the disappointment, and the defeats.
You have tasted the hardships
and the frustrations.
You have seen the people,
the attractions, and lifestyles.
Then why would you want to live there?
Get out, you have no right living there.

The valley has been the place of
confusion, conflicts, fears, and doubts.
It has been the place where idlers hang out.
It has been the place where the voice
of God is shut out.
Why tarry there when sin
and darkness abounds?
It is the devil's work ground,
So why dare to live there when there
are better grounds?

God wants you out of the valley.
He is calling you out and up to
the mountaintop.
He is calling you out of Sodom,
calling you out from impending hell.
It's a place of destruction.
It's a place of misery and strife.
Get out of the valley before it is night.
Meet God at the top of the mountain
where He shows His face.
Get out of the valley and climb
to the mountaintop.

Get Out of Egypt

Get out of Egypt,
That's not where you belong.
You have labored in bondage long,
living on Pharaoh's land.
Get out of Egypt, it's not the promised land.
Get out of Egypt,
Egypt is not God's plan.

Get out of Egypt,
it's a foreign land.
Get out of Egypt, out from
under Pharaoh's hands.
You must resist his commands.
You must not adapt or adhere to
the customs, practices,
or principles of strange gods.

You are called out of Egypt.
You are called out of bondage.
You'll lay no more bricks.
You'll mix no more mortar.
You will gather no more straws or sticks.
Egypt's policies and practices,
you must resist.

You are coming out of Egypt
This very day, this very night.
Get out of bondage and displeasure,
you should not look back.
You have tarried there too long.
You should be in readiness
for the next flight to the promised land.

Get out of Egypt.
Onions, garlic, leeks,
and cucumbers, they're
nothing to feast on.
God's children require milk and honey,
that you must understand.
Get out of Egypt.
Get on the next flight.
You must flee and leave Pharaoh
and his people behind,
this very day or this very night.

Get Out of the Grave

Get out of the grave, why stay there?
Take off your grave clothes and leave them there.
Jesus has promised you a new and better life,
life more than you ever had before.
Get away from the graveyard, only the dead belongs there.

Get out of the grave, it's no place to stay.
Get away from the grave, don't linger near.
Put on your praise garment and position yourself for life.
Speak out against death,
Call out for life.

Get out of the grave, there's darkness there.
Get out of the grave, there's much for you to do.
Get out of the grave, get away from those that are dead.

See the nations out there, they are waiting on you.
Put on your life garment and begin to live the new life.
Take off the dead clothing, no longer do they belong to you.
Put on the new man and allow Him to speak through you.
Get out of the grave, it's a dark place.
You are alive and not dead.
There's work for you to do, work among the living and not the
dead.

Get Up, Rise Upon Your Feet

You may be knocked down
but you are not knocked out.
Get up, stand upright, and fight for your life.
Never lay down as if you are dead.
Never throw up your hand and surrender to the enemy.
Never give Him a chance to stand or trample on your head.

Get up, stand up, you are not dead.
Pick up your shield and sword,
slip on your armor,
fasten tight your breastplate,
apply faith, and start to fight the good fight again.

Be confident.
You have got the strength to get up.
Stand up.
You are not in this fight to be a loser.
You are a winner.
You are not a doubter.
You are a believer.
Get up, stand upright, and fight for your life.

Get Up

Get on your feet now.
Don't allow yourself to stay down.
Don't allow the devil to think that
he has knocked you down and out.
Get up and let him know the
fight has just begun.

Get up, it's important you don't stay down.
Get up and let the devil know he is
no match for the one in you.
You are victor.
You are an overcomer.
You are more than a conqueror, too.
Get up and show the mighty working power
of God in you.

Give Him Your Heart

After you've developed heart
strains and pains,
After you've experienced heart murmurs,
After your diagnosis says sin and shame,
It's time for surgery.

Now that you are left with
life-threatening defects,
it's time for you to go to the Lord
and lay your problems at His feet.
It's time for you to seek relief.

Give the Lord your heart, let Him heal it.
Give the Lord your heart, let Him keep it.
The day you do, you'll find rest and peace.
Give Him your heart, let Him work on it.
Give Him your heart, He'll make it whole.

Give Him your heart, He'll treat it right.
Give Him your heart, body, and soul.
Give Him your heart in exchange
for His kingdom.
Give Him your heart, let Him heal it.

Give It to God Now

Give him your sorrow, He'll give you joy.
Give Him your troubles, He'll give you peace.
Give Him your life, He will turn it around.
Give Him your cares and your burdens to bear.
Give it to Him now.

Don't wait until there's a problem to think about Him.
Don't wait until you are burdened and overwhelmed with sin.
Begin right now to look to Him and give Him your everything.
Hold fast to the message that He brings and trust always in Him,
for nothing in life will be strange or difficult for Him.
It's up to you to be obedient and cast all your cares and burdens on
Him.

When we give Him our challenges,
we can be confident that solution He will bring.
When we surrender our all to Him,
we can be sure He will arrest, curve, and turn them around.
When we allow Him to take up those hard, harmful, and unusual
things,
we can expect Him to subdue, change, and make them good and new.
When we give Him the things that would beset us,
then we can stand back and watch Him change them.

So let's give Him the weight of our burdens and cares.
Let's give Him the sorrows we bear.
Let's give Him everything we cannot and shouldn't handle.
Let's give them to Him, He will gladly take and handle them.

Give Me Hands

Give me hands that will reach out to others.
Not just my sisters and my brothers,
but hands that reach around the corners
and beyond the bends and borders.
Hands to hold and caress the wounded,
the condemned, and the rejected.

Give me hands that are opened not folded,
unless to warm and comfort the wounded
and the brokenhearted.
But, first, show me how to hold them close
and to embrace them with your enduring love.

Give me the hands that lend
the hand that gives from the heart
and into the bosom.
The hand that does not hold back when
it's time to give.

Give me the hands that will not collapse,
but hands that can be held up high.
Hands that shoot up to the skies
to point the way to paradise.
Give me hands that are willing and diligent.
Hands that are strong to work according
to God's plans and purposes.
Give me hands and let me diligently work with them.

Give Me to Drink

I am thirsty,
Thirsty for the Word, thirsty for God.
Give me to drink that which will quench my thirst,
give me that which my soul desires,
that which my soul longs and thirst for.
Give me to drink.

I thirst, dear Lord, I thirst.
My soul desperately within me thirsts.
Give me to drink, let me drink
as one who is thirsty and desperately needs to drink.
Let me drink, dear Lord, let me drink.
My soul within me cries out for the living water.
Fill me up, I need to drink.

Give me to drink.
Refresh my soul, I pray.
Give me fresh living water
that I will never thirst again.
Give me much to drink,
I am hungry and thirsty.
I want to feel brand-new,
An overflow will not be too much.
My soul yearns for the overflow.

With the living water, fill my cup.
Keep me free from dehydration.
Keep me safe from pain and heartache.
Keep me free from thirst. Give me to drink.
Give me to drink. Give me to drink.
Give me to drink today.

Go Ahead

Go ahead and call me names.
Go ahead and try to defame me.
Go ahead insult and try to intimidate me.
Your effort will bring you noting, it will be done in vain.
My Christian belief and conviction,
I will not halter, change, or apologize for.
I stand firm, steadfast, and anchored in
Jesus Christ, the Son of God.

Go ahead and try to wrongly accuse me.
Spread all the lies about me, my religious belief, and affiliation.
I will wear it as a badge of honor.
You will not deter or scare me. You will only
help to strengthen and motivate me.
I am for the promotion of the Gospel of Jesus Christ
and I am not ashamed.

I am not ashamed of that mighty, honorable, and noble name.
So go ahead and abuse me all you think you can.
You will not be able to hinder or prevent me.
I will not be shaken.
I am strong.
I am abiding in God.

Go ahead, keep up the smear campaign.
Keep on fighting against me.
Keep on hating and demonizing me.
Nothing will break me or make me halter my decision.
I will not bow.

Go

"Go," He said into all the world.
"Go without looking back.
I am the truth, the life, and the only true way.
Go deep into the lands.
There are people waiting for you.
Go to the hills, mountaintops, plains, and rocky terrains,
And find and bring out the lost.
You don't have to fear, for lo, I'm with you always.
Go on to the highways, byways, and hedges.
Go in my name.
Go in my strength.
Go with your whole heart.
Go, go I say.
Go tell my people
I am the Lord their God.
Go without your purse.
Go with your Bible in your hand.
Go with my word in your mouth and in your heart.
Go and spread the good news all over this earth."

God Is Able to Do All Things

There is absolutely nothing that God cannot do.
The hard, the complex, the small,
the great, and the extraordinary, too.
To experience His supernatural working power,
Release your faith in Him and call on Him.
You will experience not only His love, but
His awesome working wonder.

When the doctor says there is cancer,
God has the perfect cure as the answer.
When a tractor-trailer is blocking your way,
call Him up, He will find the right wrecker to move it away.
If you notice that your wine is running out, check with Him.
He is the master brewer and converter of water into fine wine

When you find that you are blind,
be still and know that He's a healer and sight giver.
He is the all-knowing,
All powerful, compassionate miracle worker and King.
He will expel the darkness, if you will let Him.
He is the light supplier in a dark world.
There is no darkness that He cannot expel
and no light that He will not brighten or restore.

When you get caught up in a storm,
declare His words to obtain a calm.
If you have problems and issues you cannot solve,
reach out and touch His garment now.
If, like Lazarus, you are laying dead,
He alone has the power to raise even the dead.

If with demons you are possessed,
He will chase them out of you and back into hell.
When you've toiled all night and no fish you hook,
it's time to cast your net on the other side of the brook.
If you have lost your way, call on Him for the salvation way,
for there is nothing that He cannot do,
And now it's your time to try Him, too.

God Is Bigger and Mightier than All of These

Bigger than our adversities,
Bigger than needs, expectations, and dreams.
Greater than our thoughts and feelings,
mightier than all the complexities of life,
Bigger and mightier than all of these.

God Sees You

Even while you are in the belly of the whale,
He sees and knows you by name.
He sees and knows when you will get out from
the dungeon underground.
His eyes are fixed in every place,
nothing is able to escape His gaze.
His eyes triumphs over everything.
There is no place that you may hide.
He watches closely at all times.

God has eyes that move to and fro,
eyes that move to every place you go,
even in the depth of hell.
His eyes doesn't narrow but
sharpens and brightens instead.

God sees everything you do,
whether it be great or small
The tiniest thing doesn't slip from His eyes,
He has eyes that spans the world
and look the mountains up and down.
Don't try to hide your wrong or right.
With observant eyes, He sees them, every one.

Goliath of Gath

Goliath of Gath was a strong and tall man, we are taught.
He was a giant, in fact, who boasted his strength.
As you will recall, the Philistine people made him
their champion and all.
With helmet of brass, a coat of mail, a staff,
a spear, and a shield in hand, he paraded the land.
Hurling insults from his top of the mountain,
for that was his way to defy, intimidate,
and provoke the Israelite people.

King Saul and his men, while being dismayed and afraid,
couldn't find one willing to confront and kill this man.
Goliath was convinced that he had the power to
disarray the Israel's army, kill their people, and take the land.
So he mocked and ranted, his words were harsh,
derogatory, bitter, and brutal.

As David, a young shepherd boy, came along,
he heard the sharp, ugly words of the giant man.
It made him angry and rather mad.
David's brother tried to dissuade him,
but David felt threatened and violated, as the giant paraded.
He realized there was a cause and he was the person to answer the call.
He rehearsed his resume and, needless to say,
he remembered that with his bare hands he had killed a bear and a lion.

As He stood before the uncircumcised giant that awesome day,
with five stones in his hand, Goliath swore
but didn't realize that he was swearing his own life away.
Goliath was overconfident in himself, he boasted
his strength, and promised to give David's body to the birds
of the air and the beast of the field. David, in the meanwhile,
must have silently prayed, then aimed at the giant's
forehead and took his life away.

This is a powerful story that we all should read, then allow
ourselves to stand in the place of David, stand confidently,
stand without fear, face the giants in our way, and get rid
of them from our land and our grounds.

Go Possess the Land

A land filled with milk and honey,
A land you are called to possess.
A good land.
A blessed land.
A beautiful land.
A land to be desired.

Don't be discouraged or fearful
by the misinformed fearmongers,
deceivers, and doubters.
They say there are giants in the land,
but aren't you more than conquerors?

Don't see yourself as grasshoppers
but receive God's word and declare
yourself overcomers?
Go possess the land.
Go do according to what God has planned
and purposed for you to do.

God has given you the land,
go possess it now.
Don't wait for your adversaries
to invade or overtake you.
Go possess the land, it belongs to you.
You don't have to depend on self or strength,
God goes before you.
He knows the way.
He makes it.
You could not ask for more.

Take over, let darkness flee.
Get up and go possess that land which
God is putting in your hands.
Don't make yourself an instrument of
doubts and fears,
If God says go, go now.
Go possess the land.

Go turn the occupiers out.
If He says you will defeat
the enemies, you will.
Don't say tomorrow. Do it now.
Look not for the giants but look to the one who gives you the land.

God's Word Will Stand the Test of Time

They try to shoot it down.
They disobey and dishonor it.
They condemn and compromise it.
They even try to get rid of it.
Yet it remains quick, powerful, sharp,
and forever strong.

It will not return to God void.
It points out evil and wrongs.
It explores and exposes darkness
and evil deeds.
It embraces, it encourages,
It will stand the test of time.
It will forever stand,
You can lean on it.

Go Spread the Good News

Go spread the gospel,
Don't keep it to yourself.
Get it out on every street and
in every corner of each town.
Spread the news, don't hide it
in your house, under bushel,
or under the ground.

Go spread the gospel,
it is the good news.
Let men know that Jesus saves,
delivers, heals, and keeps.
Let sinners know that for
them He died.
Let them know that He arose
from the dead so that
they can have the new life.

The gospel is good news,
go spread it now.
Go spread it over land and over
seas and all around.
Go spread the good news of life
abundantly.
Go spread the good news,
the news about Jesus Christ.

Go Talk to God He's Waiting

God is always waiting,
waiting to hear from you.
He knows when you are broken.
He knows when you are at your wits' end.
He waits on you to call Him up
to share your burdens
and cares with Him.

He has no plans to let you down
or make you feel that you should
not have called,
instead He bids you come
and have a talk at no cost.

Whenever you think you need to talk,
it's best to go to Him.
He listens well and finds solution better
than you could have asked.

Go talk to God about all your problems.
He's the only one you can truly trust.
He'll never turn you down or share your
problems with someone else.

He is personable.
He is confidential.
He is authentic
He is wise.
You can talk to Him at any time.

Go Tell the Enemy I Have Got Sixty-six on My Side

Go tell the enemy I am fully-loaded,
I have got sixty-six on my side and ready for him.
Tell him it's always close by me and
I will not tolerate or spear him.

Go tell my enemy I will not fear him.
Not with sixty-six on my side.
With it, I am ever ready.
With it, I will be victorious.
Go tell Him I am armed and dangerous.
Tell Him that with sixty-six on my side,
I am well prepared to overpower and overthrow him.

With my sixty-six I am made alive.
I am alert and I am made aware of his activities and actions.
I have good and reliable information on him.
I am daily informed of his strategies, tricks, and plans.
And when on my knees, I can better see him.
After studying my firing instructions,
that's when I aim at him and I know I will not miss.

I will not miss my target,
for my sixty-six has been proven.
It is precise, quick, powerful, and a sharp weapon.
In all of man's findings, there has never been another like it.

So now go tell my enemy I have got my sixty-six,
and God Himself is the chief executor of it.
I am a student of His firing school and I now partner with Him.
We are working together.
He has taught me how to aim.
Go tell the enemy, I am now trigger-happy
and have made my vow that I will not lay down my armor
but will join others in taking him out.

Hail to Thee, America

Land of the bold and the free,
I salute, appreciate, and reverence thee.
Your open doors and generosity overwhelms me.

You stand blessed among the many nations.
Your red, white, and blue shine out even on dark nights.
Why should I not say "Thank you" for the blessings you share?

Thank you, America, for your unmatched courage, boldness, and
generosity.
Though you are so often criticized and ostracized, you never seem
to back down, fail to shine, or be the challenger and defender you
are called to be.

Hail, America, continue to stand tall.
Stand up for the weak and feeble, the have not, and the neglected.
Stand strong, America, by God you are divinely protected.
Hail to you, America, big brother for all.

Love to you, America, land of the bold, home of the free.
Hail to you, America, for you I pray.
Peace to you, America, may God continue to guide and protect you.
Joy to you, America, may love, peace, joy, favor,
and happiness adorn and reign over you.

Hands and Hearts Are Needed

They are the tools that God works with.
Give them to Him, let Him heal, anoint
and set them to work,
for, surely, He has work for them to do.
Hands to mold, nurture, fashion, and explore.
Hearts for acceptance, compassion,
Love, and to understand.
Hands and hearts are needed to
execute God's eternal plans.

Hands and hearts are needed
if God must work through man.
Hands and hearts are needed
if God must inspire and transform man.
Give your hands and heart to Jesus, let Him
use them to demonstrate and perform
His eternal plans.

He Bore and Did It All for You

He took on the pain you couldn't endure.
He took the cross you couldn't carry.
He accepted the shame that you couldn't bear.
He modeled the life that you couldn't live.
He bore and did it all for you.

Assaults were frequently made on Him.
Boos and jeers were hurled at Him.
He was wounded for your many transgressions.
He was bruised for your multiple iniquities.
He was despised and rejected,
yet He opened not His mouth.
He bore and did it all for you.

He took on the sins of man.
He was made to suffer and die.
He was buried among the poor and lonely.
He bore and did it all for you.
What will you do for Him?

He Gives Beauty for Ashes

He stripped me of my ugliness.
He wiped away the soot.
Anointed me down with the oil of joy,
He poured it out all over me
and gave me beauty for ashes.

He saw me wounded.
He saw me bewildered and depressed.
He saw me choked and drowning.
He saw me with the rope around my neck.
He came in and rescued me from death.

He gave me beauty for ashes
and for my confusion, He gave me peace.
He saw the misery.
He removed it all and gave me new life, His love, and joy.

He removed the roughness.
He removed the stains, the bruises, and the scars or blotches.
He removed the brokenness and the messiness.
Smoothed me over and covered me with grace
and gave me beauty for ashes.
He gave me beauty I did not deserve, and now
I am complete and whole again.

He Has My Back

He has my back because He's like that.
I don't have to arm myself with (so-called) secular protective gears.
When surrounded by enemies, I have nothing to fear.
God has my back, therefore, I have nothing to fear.

He has my back,
I am convinced about that.
He has my back in everything.
He'll keep me from being defeated or attacked.
Thank God for that, He has my back.

When it seems like hell is breaking loose,
And the devil is on top.
I don't have to worry.
I don't have to fear.
I don't have to give in.
I will not be disillusioned for I am confident of the fact.

God has my back.
He has my back.
It doesn't matter what.
He never lets me down.
He keeps himself always around.
He has my back.
He never forgets.
He never flinches.
He never loses a fight.
He has my back.

He'll Raise You Up

When you are feeling knocked down and out,
God will lift you up if you will allow Him.
He'll not allow you to stay down.
He will not allow you to be defeated or cheated.

When you are feeling that you have come to the end of your rope,
He'll not allow you to be choked or fall overboard.
When you are feeling wounded and lost,
He'll raise you up to stand on firmer ground.
He'll not let you stay down.

When you ask Him to raise you up,
He'll not turn you down.
He's always willing and ready to raise
you up from off the ground.
His arms are forever outstretched to
raise up those who have fallen down.

He Holds Back the Darkness

So that I can see,
He holds back the night to give me daylight.
He will not allow my feet to slip or to stumble,
He guides my walk.

He holds back the darkness with His powerful hands.
He makes the path sound for us to travel on.
Robbers and thieves may prowl around in the dark,
but He makes provision to cover and protect our walk.

He holds back the dark to allow the light to come in
to fulfill a purpose that nothing else can give.
He holds back the darkness.
He wrestles it into submission.

He holds back the darkness and allows light to lighten,
attract, inspire, and transform.
He holds back the darkness so that light may have its course.
He holds back the darkness so that light may triumph.
He holds back the darkness so that light could win.

He Is, Isn't He?

Like music in my ears,
the fragrance of a fresh lily.
He is like the morning dew
that's a bit of Him.

Once you get to know Him,
The sweetness you'll find.
His presence is astonishing,
It radiates and brings fullness of joy sublime.
For only love, goodness, mercy,
and beauty are attached to Him.

He never fades, fails, or falters.
He's omnipotent.
He's wise and wonderful,
yet He's compassionate, thoughtful, sweet, and kind.
He is, isn't He?

He's Coming Back

His schedule has not changed.
He will come again.
He will be on time.
His plans remain the same.
Be watchful, ready, and waiting.
He's coming back for you.

He's coming back to take you home.
If you are ready,
then you will go with Him.
If not, you'll be left behind.
So keep this in mind and be ready
when He comes,
when He comes to take you to that
place beyond the sky.

He may not come at the time you expect Him.
He could come anytime now.
Keep your heart fixed on His promises.
Keep your eyes on the glorious prize.
Be on the alert.
Be ready and prepared.
Keep looking up to the sky,
He could come at any time.

Help Me to Find My Way, Lord

Lord, please help me to find my way
as I go through the struggles of each day,
as I walk through the valley of fears and doubts.
Help me to find my way.

Help me to find the courage to
fight back the darkness,
the darkness that keeps me from seeing you.
I am prevented by the darkness.
I am challenged by it.
It is trying to hold me captive,
but I must resist and get away from it

It's dark out there.
It would seem as if the moon has hidden its face.
I can hear the wind howling and growling
and I can feel it snapping at my face.
But I am determined to fight the darkness
that I may find my way.
So help me to find my way, Lord,
help me to see your face.

He Made a Promise to Me, I Made a Promise to Him

I knew that I was being challenged
and I knew that I was living wrong.
I knew that I had to find some help.
I knew of no better place than to
go to God.

I poured out to Him my many problems.
He listened attentively, then sweetly said,
"My child, give me your life and
I will take care of your all."
That day, He made a promise to me.
And now I have found a friend in Him.
Life has changed since
He made a promise to me and I made
a promise to Him.

Yes, life was full of uncertainty.
Life was full of ups and downs.
But I have given Him my everything,
the things I once thought I owned.
My life, my wealth, and my all,
Now they all belong to Him.
I hold back nothing.
He made a promise to me and I made
a promise to Him.

Since then, I asked myself a million times,
why did I ever chose sin over Him?
I tell myself how foolish I have been.
My eyes were blinded, but now I see.
My life has become His,
He made a promise to me.
And I made a promise to partner with Him.
Oh, what a blessing!

He Makes My Heart Sings

Filled with gratitude
And bursting with His love,
marveled by His loving kindness,
He makes my heart sing.

With His joy all around me
and His promises being fulfilled,
souls being saved
and miracles being realized,
He makes my heart sings

The Pentecostal fire is burning,
but it will not prevent the sweet
sound of an abundance of rain.
It's strange things that are happening.
It is the supernatural
and it makes my heart sing
with great joy and happiness
and added gratefulness.

He Never Fails or Falters

When others fail and falter, He never will.
When others raise their hands in surrender,
He remains steadfast, confident, and strong.
When others give up and bow in defeat,
He continues to prove that He is the Almighty God.

He never fails or falters in accomplishing
His will and plans.
He never fails or falters in what He tells man
What He says He'll do.
And what He does will always be right.
He never fails or falters.
His word is His bond.
Can you understand?

He Played and Sang Me a Love Song

When I woke up this morning, no stir
was in my feet or hands.
I asked the Lord to sing and play me a love
song with a mighty beat,
He echoed the lyrics
And I recited them.
Within seconds, He had me standing strong.

He helped me to my feet when He saw
that my day was going wrong.
And now, He has me singing, stomping,
and clapping, using my voice, feet, and hands.
I am rejoicing because He has made me glad.
I have been given the music and a great love song.

Play and sing for me, Jesus,
from your love let me never depart.
Let me touch heaven and learn to play
and sing along.
Play and sing for me, Jesus.
Play and sing me your love song.

He Put It All Back Together, the Dismantled Life

He has been picking up the broken pieces of human lives.
He has been picking them up forever.
Many broken pieces,
many dismantled ones,
misfit pieces, and pieces ugly with stain,
He picked them up all the same.

He picked up the pieces that others thought were no good,
pieces that were rusty, shattered, and bore signs of disgust and shame.
He put them all back together again.
He picked up the pieces that were ruined,
pieces that showed hopelessness,
pieces that were trampled and beaten down in sin.
Those are among some of the many pieces
He shows great interest in.

He picked up the overworked and worn-out pieces,
the rejected forgotten, and abused ones.
He took the time to find them.
He took the time to reshape and remodel them.
He took the time to redeem them.
He took the time to care.

If your life is in pieces, He can fix it, too.
He can put it back together that He will gladly do for you.
He will take your broken and tattered pieces
and make them brand-new.
So give Him your broken pieces and
prove for yourself the great, marvelous,
and unmatched work that He can do.

He Saw You, He Knew You

He saw you, He knew you long before you were born,
and even before you were conceived in your mother's womb.
He knew long before all others whether you would be a boy or girl,
and even before then, He had plans for you.

He watched you as you develop your limbs and other parts.
He saw you as you floated around in the womb.
He saw you as you flail your tiny legs and arms.
He saw you even on that day when you gradually pushed
your way through the birth canal and into the world.
He saw you as your mom smiled broadly and wrapped
you in her arms.
He saw and heard you even that day when you took
your first step and uttered your first word.
He saw the joy, pride, and excitement in your parents' eyes.

He saw you as you were first taken to school.
He saw your heart race and a tear in your eye when
your mom kissed you and waved and said her goodbye.
He saw you as you took your place in that picturesque
little classroom.
He saw you as you nervously and reluctantly played
with other boys and girls.
He watched and listened as you share with others in
silence, in actions, and words.
He saw you as you try to discover and find out
about this amazing world.
He saw you as you find pleasure in some of
the many things you consider.

He saw you as you grew from a child to a teenager,
and then into young adult. He saw you as you chose profession.
He knew your motive for the choice.

He saw you as you sleep at nights, and He knew whether
you would wake in the morning light. He sees and
He knows what you will accomplish each day.
He knows the hair upon your head. He numbers everyone.
He sees and He knows all the changes in you.

He sees all the physical change in you.
He sees them, every one.
He knows the number of your days, so please understand.
He sees and He knows whether you'll live for Him or some other.
He sees the people you surround yourself with, the places you visit,
the friends you choose, and the things you do.

He sees you as you go about your assignments at home and at work.
He knows your desires.
He sees, He watches, and He knows you inside out.
What an amazing God! Have you yet to find out?

Hope Walks All the Way

All the way, she has been traveling with me.
Through the sunshine, through the rain,
through the storm, and through the calm.

Hope is her name, please understand.
Why she is such a powerful, compelling, and hopeful woman?
She does not entertain fears or despair,
or housed herself where there are doubts and dismay.

She is courageous.
She is charming, bold, and true.
She is that fierce fighter who
always believe that things will work out.
She has been a sure champion on human side.
She has fought many battles and has won many fights.
She is a supplier of strength whenever it wanes or wears out.
She provides the necessary consolation when it's running low.

Hope is a strong and consistent believer.
She commits herself to think positively in all matters.
She is always hopeful for good outcomes.
She expects situations to always get better.
She is dynamic, convincing, and compelling,
and is always willing and ready to erase fears and doubts.
In all that you do, don't leave her out.

How Dare You?

How dare you try to change those things that God has
fearfully and wonderfully made?
How dare you reject, dispute, and ignore the purpose for
which man was truly made?
How dare you try to alter God's words
and claim it's not for this age?
How dare you speak against the things that God
has blessed and called them good?
How dare you place much honor on yourself
and give little or no honor or credit to Jesus the King?
How dare you?

How dare you continue to speak ugly things, when God said,
"Let your words be seasoned with salt?"
How dare you fight against God's declarations and demands?
How dare you attribute things to Him that He didn't do or say at all?
How dare you?

You dare to stand and speak against His word.
You lie on Him.
You dare to demonize those who dare to follow after Him.
You dare to use and abuse his Holy name.
You dare to minimize and falsify His true worth and fame.
How dare you?

If you are guilty of the least of these,
I dare you stop and check yourself.
Make a right about-turn and get on the right track.
If not, then,
How dare you?

How Remarkable and Precious

How wonderful is the Lord our God
to give us all things good and wonderful,
to clothe us in our rightful minds,
to warm us with His love divine,
to keep us through the many hours of the day,
and to protect us through the long lonely nights.

How precious,
How remarkable to be a member of his flock.
To be under His tender care,
to be comforted and directed by His rod and staff,
to hear His whispers in our ears,
to be anointed with His precious healing hands and oil,
how wonderful and precious is our God!

I Am a Believer

I believe in the Word of God.
I am a believer.
I believe that the Word is well, alive, and strong.
It speaks, it enlightens, it satisfies.
I am persuaded.
I am convinced.
I am compelled.
I am assured.

I am a believer.
I believe in the Word of God.
I believe it gives life and light.
I believe it is powerful and strong.
I believe it heals, delivers,
Captivates, and empowers.
I believe in the Word of God.

I believe that the Word is quick,
Quicker than lightning,
Quicker than quicksand.
I believe it is sharp, sharper than a razor
or any two-edged sword.
I believe it reaches heart.
It takes over. It dominates.
I believe it is God's message to man.
I know it is the bread of life to me.

I Am Persuaded

I am convinced.
I have concluded
I am a child of the King
and nothing, absolutely nothing,
shall separate me from His love.

I am persuaded and I am thrilled.
Nothing shall separate me from Him.
I have been offered a new life and I accept.
It's no longer a secret I am His.
He gave me reason to live.

I am persuaded.
I am fully convinced.
The things He has done to keep me alive,
all that He has been through,
He made me believe.
He made me receive.

I Believe

I believe in the God above and the work He has done.
I believe in the creation story, the garden of Eden,
and the actions of Adam and Eve.

I believe in God the Almighty that He's the Father of glory.
I believe in the Trinity—the Father, Son, and Holy Spirit.
I believe in Jesus Christ that He died and rose again.
I believe He paid the price to set mankind at liberty.

I Belong to Jesus

Oh, what a wonderful thing,
being connected to Him,
being under His wings,
It is a privilege.

I belong to Jesus.
I am not my own.
I am under His will, command, and control.
There I will abide until He calls me home.

I belong to Jesus.
Every part of me.
I have surrendered it all, nothing will I withhold.
I belong to Him from my head down to my toes.

If

If, indeed, for abundant life you seek, look into these.
For if you claim to be a Christian and not studying your Bible,
you are on your way to become biblically ignorant.
If you refuse to be persecuted for righteousness,
you will be approved for doing wrong.
If you are not walking in the Word, then you are running into sin.

If you are not awakened unto righteousness, then you
are sleeping with the enemy called sin.
If you are not abiding in the Word of God, then be sure
you are departing onto the road of disobedience.
If you are not looking into the scriptures, then
you are a blind searching in the darkness.

If you claim to know the Word and you are not
speaking it or sharing it, you are being dumb and selfish.
If you claim to be a Christian leader and not leading
men into light, then you are allowing them to follow
you into hell and its darkness.
If you are not on the road leading to heaven, then you are
on the path heading to hell.

If you claim to be wise and you are not exercising wisdom,
then you are working out in foolishness.
If you are making excuses for wrongs, then
you are a compromiser, sympathizer,
and embracer of evil and wickedness.

If you are a hater of Righteousness, then you are a lover of sin.
If you are unprepared for heaven, then you are prepared for hell.
If you are not an overcomer, then you are an underachiever.
If you are not a friend of Christ, then you are an enemy of God
and a friend of the devil.

If I Must Live

Let me not choose to live like everybody else,
but let me consciously and deliberately choose to
live only for Jesus Christ the King.
Let not riches, pleasure, or fame confuse, control,
or consume me, let it not be the major focus of
my life but rather let me live in strict obedience
and love of the Word of God. Let me esteem
God's word more than my necessary food.
Let it not depart from my mouth,
but let me meditate in it night and day.

If I must live, let me not live spending my
time chasing after recognition, admiration, or
the applaud of men, but rather let my time be
spent in praising, honoring, and adoring
the Lord God and Him only.

If I should face opposition or adversity of any kind,
Lord, let me handle it with decency and utmost
dignity, knowing that I am not the first neither
will I be the last. But God will not give me
more than I can bear.

If I must live, let me not live selfishly but selflessly
live respecting myself as well as others.
Let me not condemn or ridicule anyone.
Let me not compromise, try to halter, or reject what
God has approved or planned.

Let me not live forgetting whose I am or where
I am coming from.
Let me live knowing that life is short, it will
not last forever, and Jesus will return.
Let me not live in regret but live and die leaving
great footprints, hand marks, and a legacy of happiness
as an inheritance for generations to come, even
very long after I am gone.

If Tomorrow Comes without Me

If tomorrow comes without me, think not
of me in sorrow or in pain.
Hold not yourself guilty that I am gone ahead of you.
Don't worry, it will not be your fault.
Don't spend your time crying and grieving over me,
I did not live in vain.
I have lived my life well.
Don't think about me as dead, I live on,
but I leave the shell behind.
I have traded my flesh for a spiritual and permanent robe.
I have left my residence for a better and glorious one.
I have exchanged the old residence for a new
and better place where life never ends.

If tomorrow comes without me,
think not of me as absent or missing in action.
Just keep me in mind
I am still living, enjoying my new life with friends
and family and Jesus Christ.
Therefore, don't speak of me in the past.
I am alive and doing well.
You keep healthy. If possible, live peaceful,
make your life easy, and, most of all, worthwhile.
Enjoy the company of friends and loved ones
And always remember to share Jesus Christ.

If tomorrow comes without me, have no doubt, I am not lost.
To find me, you will have to get to that place where I now reside.
To get there, you must keep in close and
direct contact with the shepherd-man.
He watches over His sheep and none ever get lost.

I Have an Attorney

He chose to represent me in every legal matter.
He argues my case, pleads my cause,
each time that my back is up and against the wall.
After all, He is the best in life's matters.
He answers to my every call.
He is incredibly wise, good, and smart.
He never loses a case or a matter.
He is ridiculously competent.
He is undeniably, unbelievably excellent.

He is the powerhouse behind every case.
He makes everything simply easy.
He instructs, directs, and guides with wisdom, dignity, and grace.
He is the master of my fate.
He has my well-being at heart.
He is thoughtful, He is confident, He is focused, He is kind.
With all He has done for me, He never charges me a dime.

He is the greatest of attorneys.
A hater of sin.
A lover of people.
An advocate for what's right.
An advocate who makes no mistake.
He doesn't take life's business as a game.
He knows what will be the outcome of every matter.
He represents with integrity and honor.
And, oh, it's my greatest pleasure to recommend Him to you.

I Know a Man

I know a man, maybe you know Him, too.
An exceeding, extraordinary, exceptional man.
He walks this earth.
He travels to every city, village, and town.
He knocks on every door.
Some people choose to invite Him in,
Others close their doors on Him.

He knows each family by their full name.
He knows their occupation, too.
He's never aggressive, pushy, or rude to anyone.
He's always charming.
He's always a gentleman.

The man I know, He's familiar with animals great
and small, birds, fishes, and everything that flies, walks, or crawls.
The man I know is always busy but never seem tired,
Even though He doesn't go to bed at nights or take naps in the day.
His duty list is always tall, it has a beginning but lacks an ending.
He does the most amazing things, although some people
seem not fond of Him.
He is awesome in all His works and deeds,
yet there are some who does not approve of Him.
He's the most amazing man I know, although there
are many who may not think so.

He has a great and unusual understanding of everything.
He is aware of all things.
He's never surprised about anything.
He has only good reason to undo some things.
This world could not exist without Him.

The man I know is always good, wise, and kind.
He will always stand out in my mind
Because He brings me joy.
He brings me peace.
This man I know is Jesus Christ, and
I can't live my life without Him.

I Have Great Expectation

I am expecting a miracle.
A miracle soon, a miracle indeed.
It will be a miraculous moment
when this miracle reaches me.

What a remarkable sight this will be!
As the power of God descends on me,
A miracle will come forth for the world to see.
A miracle that God has promised to me.

My miracle is on its way.
I am awaiting its arrival.
I have received the notice
and have read the contents of it.
I have received clearance to take it
and I know I am feeling the vibes.

My confidence level has been elevated.
My faith has been restored since
God provided me with the revelation
that He will restore all that the
enemy has stolen from me.

I know my God is up to something
even bigger and wonderful.
I will pray, exercise faith
and confidence, and patiently wait
on Him.

In the Garden of Love

Everything spells love.
There are always fresh fruits, vegetables, flowers,
and blooming trees.
But most precious and there to be found
are wisdom, knowledge,
and the understanding of God.
Joy, peace, faith, meekness, and patience
are the petals ever dancing in space.
There they abode and abound.

In the garden of love, there God entertains
and His handiwork is forever displayed.
He often invites the birds, the butterflies,
the sunlight, the rain,
the rainbow, and, of course, some little friends
who so often wants to peep at or greet
all the beautiful people of this wonderful place
loom in the garden of love.

The garden of love is an attractive and sacred place.
It's an amazing art gallery emboldened
with promoting grace and mercy.
It's God's own place.
No unwelcome man or beast will ever be found
hanging around there.

It's a musical city and a paradise of peace.
The music is compelling. It's appealing.
It is sweet.
It is refreshing.
And only to be found in the garden of love,
the unique place.

In the Path of Righteousness

That's where he leads,
Adversity will not triumph.
Righteousness will prevail.
In the path of righteousness,
that's where we stand to receive.

In the path of righteousness,
that's where we are permitted to walk.
The devil and his cronies will not come along
because it's the path of righteousness
that leads to glory land.

In the Valley of the Shadows

There, illusions thrive and doubts arise
But fear no evil.
Shadows are not alive.
God is by your side.

In the valley of shadows, loneliness dwells.
Death is mirrored and confusion swells.
But, fear not, God is ever present.
He's ever near.

Fear no evil, though death be around you.
God will protect you from the terrors
and the arrow of the shadows.
Fear no evil, for fear is not of God.

In the valley of the shadows, even there He walks.
He provides protection for all who ask.
Even in the valley of the shadows,
He triumphs over the dark.

In the Waiting Room

There this Master Surgeon and Balm in Gilead sits.
There He provides counsel to all who come.
He doesn't rush business.
He is diligent, He's patient, He's humble,
He's just and fair.

He performs with great care and utter grace.
He is ever skillful.
His talents are rare and cannot be compared.
His works and deeds speak volume about Him.
And that's why we all should aspire to be more like Him.

If you are afflicted, sick in mind,
body, or soul, go meet with the Great Physician
and Balm in Gilead.
He is waiting there for you.

In the Waiting Room The
Great Physician Sits

There, He'll wait for you.
Some come to give birth, some for healing
and deliverance, and others for
diagnosis and for prescription refills too.

Jesus is the one awaiting them all in the waiting room.
He accepts all calls, none go unnoticed
or unanswered at any time at all.
He writes prescriptions. He fills them, too.
There are no charges for His service, major or minor,
Not even a penny or two.

In the waiting room, this quiet place,
there the Great Physician waits.
He is never absent from duty or too busy to attend to a sick.
He is on all shifts.
Neither has He ever misdiagnosed a case
or been late to attend to a sick.
He sits at the head of the prescription counter
and always greets with a smile.
In the waiting room, there Jesus you'll find.

Into the Light

On to the path of darkness, I wandered.
In the wilderness of life, I found myself.
There I was blocked, attacked, and persecuted.
There I realized I was lost.
And there I learn how
much disobedience cost.

The lessons were tough. They were real,
they were rough.
The message was just and the price was much.
I had no one to blame and no place to go.
Now surrounded by darkness,
Overwhelmed by fears, doubts,
and death, ready to take me out.
I sought for help, I cried out to Jesus Christ.

He showed up and, though blinded by darkness,
I reached my hands out to Him.
From out of the darkness, I touched Him.
I slowly arise
and into the light I soon arrived,
but not without a struggle,
not without a fight.
Thank God I have found Him.
Thank God I am out of the darkness
and now into the light.

I Say to Today

I say to today, you are mine.
I hold you in my hands.
What I do with you is left up to me and God.

You are God's gift to me.
Last night when I went to bed,
I did not know that I would wake up to see you.
Now I must wrap my arms around you and tell you,
"I am grateful for you."

I am most grateful for you.
My intention is to use you for good.
I will not allow anything to get between me and you.
I say to you, "You are a blessed day,
and I am glad to be alive."
You are mine. I will honor you
with thanksgiving and the fruits of my lips.

I will work and be joyful in you.
I will not waste any part of you.
You are for purpose, you are an
eventful time in my life.
You are the day many did not get to see.
You will provide me with experience
I did not get yesterday.
I say to you I must love and treasure you.

I say to today, "You are unlike any other day in my life.
You are a grand opportunity in which to praise God."
My eyes, I will keep steadfast on the Maker and Creator of you,
to the One who gave you to me.
I say, "Thanks." And, again, I say to today, "I will rejoice in you.
You are mine.
I am grateful for you."

I Speak to My Mountain

I speak to my mountain.
I command it to move out of my way.
I speak to my mountain.
I declare, decree, and demand it to fall
and disappear into the sea.

I speak to my mountain.
I tell it what God says in Saint Mark eleven
and verse twenty-three.
I boldly tell my mountain I refuse to have it
blocking my way.
I tell my mountain that I will not tolerate
stumbling blocks in my way
when God tells me to cast them into the sea.

When I speak the faith word God
puts in my mouth, my mountain will not act another day.
No mountain is too mighty to fall to the ground.
No mountain is too high to climb over.
No mountain is too strong to crumble.
When I speak to my mountain, it will crumble and fall.

It's Not Enough

It's not enough to say you are a Christian,
if Christ is not the main purpose of your existence.
It's not enough to say you know Him,
if you do not have a relationship with Him.
It's not enough to call Him Lord, if He's not master over all.
It's not enough to say amen, if you didn't pray in agreement.
It's not enough to make the rules,
if you yourself are not willing to abide by them.
It's not enough to talk the talk, if you are not willing to walk the walk.
It's not enough to ask for healing, if you lack the confidence in
receiving.
It's not enough to ask for forgiveness,
if you are not first willing to forgive others.
It's not enough to read the Word, if you are not willing to live by it.
It's not enough to claim that you know the truth,
if you are not speaking and exercising it.

It's Not Too Late for God

It's not too late for the sun to shine.
It's not too late to turn the tide.
It's not too late to speak to the wind.
It's not too late for the calm to set in.
It's never too late to call upon God.

It's not too late for Him to show his face.
It's not too late to win in His race.
It's not too late for Him to give grace.
It's not too late for you to make things right.
Whether it is day or night, call on Jesus Christ.
He'll show himself strong.
It's not too late.

It's Time to Give Birth

It's time to push,
push as hard as you can.
Birth pains are excruciating,
intense, and severe,
but you can survive if you push
and do not fear.

It's time to give birth
after you have labored long and hard.
It's time to show what you've wished
and labored for,
so go ahead and push.
Push and bring forth for greatness.
Bring forth for joy and success.
Bring forth for changes.
Bring forth to illuminate.
Push and bring forth to transform and bless.

You are destined to bring forth,
So push with intensity.
Push with expectation.
Push with jubilation.
Push as hard as you can.
It's time to give birth.
Take it not for granted, the
life placed inside of you.
Take it not for granted that
you are called to give birth.

It's Time to Check with Him and Give Him Your Load

Are you bewildered?
Are you overstressed?
Are you disillusioned?
Are you burdened and depressed?

Don't let this continue.
Don't let it eat at your soul.
Don't let it foster into bitterness.
Turn to God.
Let Him take over.
Let Him help you out.
It's time to check and give Him your load.

I Will Keep Searching

Until I find Him,
for He's the one and only valued treasure
that man should search for.
I must keep searching until I find Him,
for He's the way that I must go,
He's the rock that I must lean on,
The light that I must seek,
The truth that I must know,
And the life that I must live.

If I search fervently,
I will surely find Him
when I seek for Him with my whole heart,
soul, and mind.
If I seek diligently, I will find Him.
If I seek expectantly, I will find Him,
for He's all I need.
I will search until I find Him,
search and desperately long for.

I must seek and search until I find Him,
for He's the keeper of my life.
I will pursue Him and I will find Him.
I will find Him when I seek.
I will give my eyes no sleep
until I find the one my soul seeks.

I Will Not Be Silenced

I will speak out for the world to hear me.
I will not be silenced.
I will speak for Jesus Christ my Lord.
I'll not be silenced no matter how hard they try.
I have been given a message with life and death attached.
I'll rise up and speak it loud.
I'll let the people know that Jesus Christ offers eternal life.
I will share the news that
the wages of sin is death, but the gift of God is eternal life.

Though some may reject it,
Though some may try to ignore it,
I will not be silenced.
I will let them hear it.
The world must not be denied the truth,
even if they hate to hear it.
I will not be silenced.
I will speak out for God.
I will let the world know that Jesus offers life.
I will let the world know that whosoever will can have it, too.

It Shall Surely Come to Pass

Every word that the Lord has spoken,
Every promise that He has made,
it shall come to pass
and man shall know that which He says He'll do, He'll do.
It was so in the beginning and so shall it be in the end.
It shall come to pass and all eyes shall see it
and all flesh shall behold it.
Even them that are blind will see and hear it
and many will be in awe about it,
so keep your focus
for there shall be a performance
and the Lord God has said it.

Jesus Leads

He leads out of sorrow into joy.
He leads out of storm into calm.
He leads away from destruction unto a safe place.
He leads out of darkness unto perfect light.
He leads out of the night into day.
He leads as the good shepherd.

He leads onto the path He wants us to go,
onto the pathway where streams of
living water flows.
He leads through the hills and valleys
where we are afraid to go.
He leads in triumph and with authority.

He leads with confidence.
He leads with love.
He leads with patience
and understanding, too.
He leads with integrity.
He leads as the good leader.

He leads from condemnation into redemption.
He leads away from sin into righteousness.
He leads away from death into everlasting life.
Thank God He leads.

Joy Comes in the Morning

After a long night of battle,
after a long night of strife,
after a long, dark night of disappointment,
here comes joy at last.

Joy comes with it glorious changes.
It comes loaded with good news.
She never allows Love, Faith, and Hope to leave her side,
she brings them out, too.

She comes in the morning to start your day right and new.
She comes with the blessings that only God can give.
The night may be troubling,
but you can always look forward to morning when Joy arrives.

Joy comes in the morning.
She brings great favors and blessings.
She lightens up the skies, she brightens up faces.
She comes to change circumstances.
She comes with fresh supplies.
Joy comes in the morning to refresh, strengthen,
and brighten up human lives.

Keep Not Silent

Let your voice be heard.
Keep not silent.
Let the Word of God be known.
Ye who say you know God.
Ye who say He's your God.
Ye who say you love and adore Him.
Keep not silent.
Speak out for His name's sake.
Keep warning and informing.
Speak the Word not just in your house.
Hide it not on the shelf or under the bed
but preach it, live it, and teach it.
Let man know what it's all about.
Keep not silent and let evil flourish.
Help to rid the earth from it.
Subscribe no more to the devil's works and deeds.
Let him know has been dead wrong.
Speak out against wrongs.
Speak out against sin in the land.
Stand strong even in the face of tyranny.
Hold not your peace day or night.
God will always be on your side.
Keep not silent.

Lend Your Hands and Your Voice

To change the world and to do good,
get active,
participate in doing good,
share your gifts and your talents,
lend your hands and your voice to bring a soul to light.
And changes in this land
Get to the byways and hedges and invite
and call out to the lost and destitute.

Life Is a Loan

Life is a loan,
the lender is God.
A loan to have,
to love, and to cherish.
A loan with a silent secret expiry date.
Guard it well,
don't gamble with it

Life is a loan with a high interest rate.
Plan how to use it.
Never gamble with it.
You can achieve great satisfaction from it.
Be very wary not to borrow against it,
Now that you have it

Life is a loan, invest in it.
Only what you put in, you can take out.
Never abuse it.
Always take into account that you are blessed to have it.
Always take into account that God is the creator of it.
Therefore, use the manual well. It will advise
you how to protect it well.

Life is a loan.
Live it well.
Let it worth it.
Don't waste it.

Let Down Your Net

Let it down deep into the water.
Let it down confidently.
Cast your net on the right side,
There is a big catch awaiting you.

If for fish you look, it's always close to you—
in your home, the street corner, and in your schoolroom, too.
There are fishes all around you,
so do what God commands you to do.
Let down your net, there's always a catch awaiting you.

Don't fish without expectation.
Don't fish in fear and doubts.
Fish in faith and confidence,
cast your net wide and deep,
let it down, and watch the tide even as it ebb and flow.

Let your net down into the water
and allow the bait to attract.
Let faith guide you, patience have its course.
And the eyes, voice, and hands of God watch, propel, and keep you.

Let's Live Our Lives

Life is precious and priceless, indeed.
Let's enjoy it.
Let's preserve it
It is real,
let's live it.
Let it shine.
Let it tell a memorable story.

Treasure life,
it comes from God.
The devil will do everything to rob you of it,
but endeavor to live it well. Let it reflect
God's doings in it.
Let it show daily that He is in the center of it.

Life is sweet and valuable,
Let's take good care of it.
Let's not devalue it.
Let's live it honorably,
reverently, and sincerely.
Let's live it victoriously.
Let's live it for Jesus Christ.
It is a precious prize and gift.

Let Me Dance

Play me the music, let me dance.
Play skillfully that which creates a glorious song and commands a
dance.
Transport me on my feet into your presence, Lord,
and let my praise transform me into a magnificent dancing swan.

Anoint my feet and let me glide.
Let my presentation be to your absolute delight.
Let no obstacle stand in my way, and if so, let me leap over them, I
pray.
Let me dance intoxicated with your love and embalmed in praise to
you.
Let me worship you with my best dance.

Oh, let me dance to express thanks.
Let me dance above the stars.
Let me jump, leap high, and fall into your arms.
Let me dance and touch your face.
Guide my steps, never let me stumble or fall.

Allow me to dance and never stop.
Allow me to rejoice, for you have made me to dance.
Let me lift up my voice unto you as
I dance to the music of the greatest love song.
Let me dance with lifted hands.
With my whole being, let me dance and say thanks.

Let me dance for you, dear Lord.
Let me clap my hands in praise.
But most of all, let me dance from my heart.
Let me dance like David danced.
Let me dance till the light of day.

With my dance, let me worship you.
With my dance, let me salute you.
While I dance, let there be a holy stir in man.
Let me dance triumphantly.
Let my dance be a glorious dance.
Let me dance, dear Lord, let me dance.

Living on the Edge

Creating an atmosphere
being made easy to accept anything.
Things may give an appearance that it is well
and good, but when viewed in the light of God, it is not.
Read the signs of the time and
Remove yourself from that spot.
Already, you've wandered too far out on to the edge.
There, you are dangerously situated.
You are at risk.
You are close to falling into hell.

Living on the edge is taking a risk to the extreme.
Wandering out onto the edge is crazy
and presumptuous, indeed.
It is dangerous, it is outrageous, it is buzzard, it is unwise.
It's more like setting up one's self to do something
awful, insane, and wrong
It's more like trying to commit what is known as suicide.
Living on the edge is living without hope itself.
Living on the edge is putting your life in the wrong hands.

Living on the edge, oh how dangerous.
Living on the edge, you are prone to stumble.
Living on the edge is setting up yourself to fall.
Living on the edge is being ready to say your
final and last goodbye.
Living on the edge is positioning yourself for death.

Come away from the edge, God is calling you.
Come away from the edge.
You may not see the danger yourself
because you are surrounded by darkness.
You are blinded.
You are vulnerable.
You are apt to fall over any time.
Please get away from the edge,
Get away now.

Lonely Days

Lonely days are marked days of our lives.
They are full of sorrows.
They are the days when one's heart breaks and cries.
The days when tears roll mercilessly from your eyes.
But those days are gone.
Gone never to come again.
Gone to a place out of this world.

I watched as the morning opens its eyes.
I watched as sun rises in the skies.
The moon and the stars kiss darkness goodbye.
That's when I tell the lonely days goodbye.

Lonely days are over.
Joyful days are here to stay.
Lonely days were haunting days,
they would not let you laugh or pray.
But they have disappeared.
They are gone very far from here.
Now I hold fast to brighter and better days.

Lonely People

They are found everywhere.
They go through life living in the land of despair.
Lonely, heartbroken, and shedding woeful tears,
Lonely people are sorrowing people.
Lonely people are lacking for love.
Lonely people are crying out for acceptance.
They, too, want to belong.
Can't you see or hear them?

Make a Quick U-Turn If Going the Wrong Way

If you see you are going in the wrong direction,
make a quick U-turn and go the way you belong.
Don't be stubborn,
don't be foolish, turn around and go the right way.

Get away from the wrong path, although it may seem smooth and
pretty fast.
Don't be deceived or be carried away by the beautiful green trees, scenic
landscape, or the awesome flow of traffic getting in and out of town.
Aim only for the right way.
U-turns are sometimes difficult to make.
However, make that which will save you from embarrassment. Do
it for your life's sake.

Make a quick U-turn when you see you are on the wrong road.
Make a U-turn because it's worth it.
Make it for your life's sake.
Be brave and wise.
Make it before you find it's too late.

My Body

My body is the temple of the Holy Spirit, therefore,
tumor, growth, and high blood pressure
have no business in it.
With every breath I take, God's Word restores my body.
That which God has not planted in me must be
dissolved and rooted out.
Every organ and tissue in my body must function
in the order and perfection in which it was made.
I forbid my body to be deceived in any way.
In Jesus's name.

Not Again

I can hear the pow, pow!
I can hear the cries.
I can hear the sirens wailing day and night.
I can hear the groans and moans of the victims
coming from where they lie,
echoing throughout the night.
Oh God, not again!

Not again.
Let it not be.
No more shedding of innocent blood.
No more senseless killing.
No more attack, insanity, and disobedience in our land.
No more chaos and disasters.
No more hateful, poisonous, hateful rhetoric.
Oh God, not again, please let it stop.

Bad things happen every day,
even to good people.
Natural disasters require no permission.
But senseless and irresponsible behavior
has no right to become the norm or order of our day.

Not again.
The enemy should/will not have his way.
Not again should we accept it.
It's time to reject it.
It's time to seek answers.
It's time to humble ourselves and pray about it.
It's time for it to stop.

Not So

You will not have me, devil, or any member of my family.
For, as for me and my family, we will serve God.
You will not have me, devil, not when in God I trust.
You will not have me, devil, not when I know who and what you
really are.

You have tried to take over my body.
You have tried to rob me of my peace of mind.
But you will not have me, devil, no matter how hard you try.
You will not have me, devil, not my family or I.
Jesus Christ has already been the eternal sacrifice.

Devil, I serve you notice.
I serve you strict warning, too.
Don't try to come after me.
I am no longer scared of you.
I have Jesus living in me and He has promised to
keep me safe and free from you.

Not Too Damaged for the Kingdom

Even though you may be well damaged,
even though someone may have told you so,
even though you may have good reason to believe it,
you are wanted for kingdom's service.
Inquire within, you will be accepted and not rejected.

You are not too damaged for the kingdom,
even though you may be feeling so.
Quit telling yourself that you are unfit and unwanted,
God is not looking for the good and perfect.
He has purpose and plans for broken and damaged lives, too.

God cares about the lives of people.
He knows how to make them new.
He knows how to restore damaged pieces.
He never worries about the damage because
He knows what to do.
You are not too damage for the kingdom.
There's still something that He can do with you.

On Eagle's Wings

Fly me on eagle's wings,
let me take to the skies.
This has been my dream.
This will be my heart's delight.

Fly me over the ocean,
far above the palm and oak trees.
Fly me over the tallest buildings,
I want to touch the heavens.
I want to touch the starry skies.
I want to feel the cool breeze kissing my face
and stroking my arms and feet.

Soar me to the mountaintop,
soar me above the clouds and don't stop.
Take me to the place where God resides.
Take me there on eagle's wings.
I want to speak with the King.
I want to say thanks to Him.
I want to touch Him.
I want to see Him face-to-face.

Dear eagle, even with you in flight, I am relaxed.
I can enjoy the flight.
And with you, I can have a good chat.
I am not afraid.
I am feeling confident, bold, and adventurous.
I know you'll land me safely.
How wonderful it is reaching from this height,
flying on eagle's wings.
Dear bird, I'm having the time of my life.

Order Your Day

Declare and decree the outcome of your day.
Put into words and actions how it should
be from beginning to end.
Put into words what you want to accomplish.
Make your utterances and confessions stand.
Order your day in faith as you pray and go along.

Order your day not just to be a good day
but an extraordinary one.
Instruct the enemy to stay out of your way.
Stick to the manuscript of the glorious book,
From it do not look.

Avoid distractions,
keep far from temptations.
Order your day into action.
Order your day and live.

There's power in God's words.
They are not empty.
They are loaded.
Speak them boldly and order your day into action.

Order your tongue to speak with authority
into each of your day.
Call forth, decree, declare, and prophesy.
Command your day from beginning to end, tell it what to do.
Establish, create, and proclaim in Jesus's name.
Give no space to the devil.
And let's not be simplistic or casual about it.

Don't allow the enemy to rob you of any part of your day.
Resist Him,
order your day, and let him go away.

Out of the Pit

Out of the pit of hell, I have risen.
Out of the pit of hell, I have climbed.
From the jaws of the dragon, I have escaped.
That's where sin had me bound and trapped.
That's where the enemy dumped me.

Out of the gutter, I have stumbled.
From the bottom to the top, I had to climb.
On solid ground, I struggled to keep my feet.
From death's angry claws, I survived,
Even in the excruciating and massive pains of life,
God in His mercy sought me out and kept me alive.

From darkness, He pulled me.
Into light, He has brought me.
From the grave, He has called me.
In to a new life, He has placed me.
I am relieved, I am freed.
Thank God for the love, light, mercy, and new life
He has bestowed on me.

Overlooked and Devalued, Not Anymore

Once upon a time, I was inclined to feel
disheartened and broken,
disappointed and distraught,
neglected and rejected,
cracked and disheveled,
beaten down and worn-out,
molested and flushed out.

But up from the grave I came
and now I encourage myself.
I tell myself,
"Self, you are fearfully and wonderfully made.
You are the apple of the most precious eyes.
You are the Lord's.
You were bought with a price.
You are the redeemed of the Lord."
And though self may not nod or verbally reply,
I am confident I am the Lord's child.

Peace

I tried to find it but it was not anywhere.
I tried to find it in wealth, fame, and fortune.
It was not there.
I tried to find it in music, movies, sex, books,
magazines, alcohol, and drugs.
It seemed as if peace had eluded me.
It seemed to have flown out to sea.
I could not find it.
It was not here or there.
It was nowhere,
not even among my family,
friends, or acquaintances.

I searched hard.
I searched long.
I searched diligently, up and down this land.
I called out for it.
It was not even in the atmosphere.
I inquired of those who claimed to own it
and wanted to offer it.
Their words were worthless, vain, and bare.

I searched almost everywhere
and came to find out it was not in the, people, places,
or things from which I seek.
But I knew I had to find it, though, it
seemed to be nowhere.

I reached out to Jesus when I heard that He offers it.
I called out to Him for that wonderful peace.
I called out loud.
I explained my need.
He brought me just what I needed
and now I have peace.
I am glad I did because now
I know He is the only one that gives
peace, perfect peace.

Pour Out from Your Precious Alabaster Box

Jesus waits on us to come in and pour out our treasures.
Pour out some of our costly and precious ointment on to others.
Pour it onto the sores and wounds of some
of the many wounded, hurting, and despondent people.

He waits for us to wash and wipe away their tears
and gently anoint their heads, hands, loins,
and feet with some of our precious ointment
coming from our alabaster box,
allowing it to seep deep into the hurting spots.

He wants us to share.
He wants us to care.
He calls us to minister love as we pour
out the sweet, precious oil from our alabaster box.

The ointment we carry may be precious and costly to us,
but He wants us to pour from it.
He wants us to meet needs with the oil from our box.
He wants us to be sensitive to the needs of others
and even in the face of criticism, objection,
and rejection. We must willingly seek to pour out
not what is worthless but that which is costly and precious.

He wants us to leave the persons we anoint
with the uncommonly warm and the sweet fragrance
coming from our alabaster box.
He wants the people we treat to know.

Yes, it will take commitment, thoughtfulness,
and compassion to pour out from our costly
and precious treasure.
It will take the hand of God to move hands,
heart, body, and souls

However, we must be determined and persuaded
to become that person meeting needs with precious
and costly ointment
flowing from our alabaster box.

And now, may the Lord raise up many
and give them the courage to willingly pour from their box.
Let them ignore the remarks of those
who would dare to speak of their association
with the neglected, the lost, and the wounded.
Let the time of pouring out be memorable
and rewarding and the results be astounding.

Pray without Ceasing

Pray with fervency.
Pray with sincerity.
Pray with determination.
Pray and never stop.
It will work effectively.

Pray believing.
Pray expecting.
Pray for changes.
Pray to God.
He can do it.

Pray until you hear from God.
Pray with passion and compassion.
Pray without ceasing.

Put On the Full Armor of God (Encouragement)

Gird up your loins,
put your full armor on,
and keep it steadfast, firm, and strongly on.
Protect yourself against the devil hiding out in the dark.
Put your full armor on, I beg and plead with you.
Leave nothing out, don't be deceived.
Put your full armor on before you step out.

Gird yourself about with the truth, the whole truth,
and nothing but the truth.
Put on the full armor of God,
put it on now.
Dress yourself as royalty.
Dress as a true soldier, indeed.
Be wise, be smart, and be appropriately attired,
wearing the breast plate of his righteousness.
Shod your feet with the gospel of peace,
put on the shield of faith,
and the helmet of salvation before you leap.

Put on the full armor of God,
take nothing for granted.
Put on the full armor,
put it on now.
Be prepared.
Put it on fast,
Be vigilant, be aware.
Be proactive, do it now.
The devil is on the loose.

Put Out the Darkness and Turn On the Light

Don't be confused and consumed by the darkness,
Turn on the light.
Don't try to walk in darkness,
Turn on the light.
Don't be entrapped by the darkness,
Let the light come in.
You'll only be deceived and strangled in the darkness
if you refuse to receive and accept the light.

There's overwhelming darkness all around.
But where there's darkness, God's light shines.
Where there's darkness, God's light abounds.
Put out the darkness and search for the light.
Push back the darkness and call in the light.
Put out the darkness and hold onto the light

Put out the darkness.
Put it away from your life.
Reach for the light, let it nullify the darkness.
Put out the darkness.
Put it out of your life.
Let it not hinder or block your vision.
Let it not cause you to stumble.
Let it not rob you of a good life.

Put Your Damaged and Broken Pieces into His Hands

Put your damaged and broken pieces into God's hand.
Put them there and watch Him work.
He delights in making over.
He excels in creative works.
Place them in His care for full service.
Leave them there and have no fear.

Let Him remold and recreate them.
Let Him restore and beautify them.
Let Him transform them for your good.,
Let Him make them over for your use again.
Put your damaged and broken pieces into God's hands.
Leave them there, He'll perform miracle
and carry out His wondrous plans in them.

Restore Me, Let Me Live Again

Give me back my life,
let me live again.
Give me back that which I have allowed
to be taken from me, that which was my
fault but not your will.
Let me realize my mistake and live for you again.

Restore to me my life, dear Lord.
Please let me live again.
Not as I choose, but as you would have me to be.
Let me live the life of you that others may see.
Let me not squander, abuse, or lose it
but Give it all back to thee.

Give me back my life, Lord, lest I live like a
despised, wounded animal, an out of control train,
or a headless man walking around.
Give me back the life you once gave to me,
Let me live again.

Say It Aloud

Say the name of Jesus.
Say it aloud and be proud.
Say it with conviction.
Say it because it's righteous.
Let it be known all about.

Say the name of Jesus everywhere you go.
Let it be your motto.
Let it be your love song.
Say it with reverence.
Say it confidently.
Say it continually.
Say it each and every moment of your life.

Say it because it's glorious.
Say it because it matters.
Say it because it's most powerful.
Say it because it's true.
Say it because there's no other name like it.
Say it aloud, *"Jesus."*

Say No

Say no to the devil.
Say no to sin.
Say no to sickness.
Just say no and live.

Say no to depression.
Say no to lack.
Say no to death and dying.
Say no to the devil's tricks.
Say no to things that bound
and try to keep you back.

Say no to adversity.
Say no and live.
Say no and do not allow sin to come in.

Set Not Your Affection on the World and Its Goods

Set not your affection on the world and its goods,
rather set it on things far up above.
Yearn, hunger, and thirst for the things that will last.
Seek for the treasures that will not rust, age, or fade with time.
Seek not for those things that will attract worldly attention and
minds,
but seek for those things that are good, godly, and kind.

Set not your affection on the world and its goods,
but rather set your affection on the heavenly prize.
Seek diligently, seek until you find.
Seek like a good shepherd would seek for a lost sheep.
Seek like a lion seeking for fresh blood and meat.
Seek like a man seeking for a precious, hidden treasure.
Seek like a cold, hungry soul would seek for warmth, food, and fire.

Set your affection steadfastly on the things of God.
Set yourself on pure love, love that is divine,
love that comes from only up above.
Waste not your time chasing down fame, riches, or pleasures,
rather get ready for a payment laid out in heaven.
Waste not your time looking for a price that is earthly right,
Rather live for Jesus Christ your eternal sacrifice.

Shaken by Fear

Shaken by your past,
put to the test,
driven by harsh circumstances,
obsessed with realities,
blinded by fears and doubts,
shaken to the core.
The world may expect you to accept it.
The world may expect you to live with it.
But you don't have to do it.

You don't have to live with fear.
There's a better way.
Don't be shaken down by fear.
Don't let it have its way.
Love conquers fear.
Choose to live for God.
Don't be shaken and disturbed.
Fear is false evidence appearing real.
Have faith in God.

Shame the Devil

Don't let him rob you of your
peace of mind.
Shut him down.
Go after his kingdom and seek to tear it down.
Shame him.
Do not play around with him.
Keep away from him.
Shame him. Shame him now.

Be a thorn in his flesh,
poison in his coffee,
a dagger in his side,
a prick in his eye,
an arrow pointing to his head,
coals of fire under his feet,
and blocks of ice in his bed.

She Gave Her All

The woman bravely stepped forward.
She laid her offering down.
She did not care what others might have
inclined to think or say of her.
It was all that she had but she laid it there
and stepped away, not even looking back.

She had an obligation she was satisfied to fulfill.
She knew in her heart she wanted to please God.
She laid her all down and knew in her heart.
she did the right thing. She gave her all.
She knew in her heart she did an honorable thing.

What remarkable person is this you are now hearing about?
A person who chose to give her all and did not doubt.
A person that sacrificed her all.
What person is this to deny herself? To make an offering
yet so small but for a good cause, knowing too well
it was the last that she possessed.
Her action that day did not go unnoticed, anyway,
for many came to find out that she gave her all away.

She gave her all, she kept nothing back.
She gave her all, even that which she lacked.
She gave her all to receive a blessing and recognition
that came only from above.
She did not stop to waver or to wane over
what she had to give.
She dedicated and graciously placed it
among the other offerings made.

That widow's mite stood out to Jesus Christ
and that which she gave was observed by the right pair of eyes.
Today it is recorded and remembered in the Book of Life.
A story that tells how to give to receive a blessing that will not hide.

Sin

The word is out. Sin has hit the number one spot.
Humans are buying it up. It's going faster than freshly baked bread.
The news media is promoting it and the world is embracing it.
It's being advertised in every news media, every state, city, and
town.
It's winning its way into our hearts, homes, schools, and streets.

It' sometimes comes in disguise, but most times it comes
dressed in glowing colors with labels very bright
and appealing to the eyes.
It's destructive, it's brazen, it's glamorous yet cold.
It's calling out to the young as well as the old and very old, too.
It is awfully bold.

It is real and it's always on the attack.
What a fiasco it has become, so popular and hardened
that many are fooled by it.
People are being drawn to it because it wears a subtle disguise.
Always seeming attractive, harmless, popular and nice.
The good news is you don't have to be a part of that.
It will destroy you if wisdom you lack.
You are living in a sinful world, it's time you realize
and acknowledge that.
Sin is destructive.

Slow Down (A Message for the Youths)

Slow down,
take your time,
you are moving too fast.
Stop a moment and check with the good book.
You are on the wrong path.
Youth doesn't mean you break the rules.
Youth doesn't mean you play the fool.

Stop racing to be on the front page or on
television headline news.
You may get there but get there dead wrong.
Stop flexing your muscles, rebelling
against the government,
your parents, and God.
Stop doing what's dangerous, sinful, and wrong.
Take heed to your ways,
use your youth well.
It will never come again.

Slow Down

People! Slow down, you are going too fast.
Slow down, you are missing the signs and the marks.
Slow down, think clearly what your action could cost.
Get out of the fast lane or you are in for a loss.
Slow down, people,
You are going to crash.

Slow down, people, slow down,
you are going too fast.
Slow down, check, you'll see that you are being arrogant,
selfish, inconsiderate, and miserable.
It's fair to exercise your rights, but please consider
and respect the rights of others.
So slow down to avoid getting yourself
or another to an eternity too early or too fast.

Slow down, people, slow down,
you are speeding.
You are going too fast.
Why go so fast when you can slow down
and better enjoy the ride and the scene?
Look at the road before you with
its beautiful shrubs, hillsides, and lush green trees.
Slow down as you go, take in some fresh air,
share a warm and generous smile.
Slow down and enjoy life

Stay in the Word

Stay in the Word of God and let the Word stay in you.
Let it be your greatest delight and let it give light to you.
Without the Word you'll be confused and deceived.
Stay in the Word and produce good seeds.

If life you seek, then on the Word you must feast.
If length of days you look, then begin to eat.
Keep in the Word and let it be your daily bread.
Feed on the Word or you will soon be spiritually dead.
Depend on the Word to lead you away from sin and hell.

Stay in the Word and let the Word stay in you.
Stay in the Word, that's the wisest thing to do.
Stay in the Word, let it guide and direct you.
Stay in the Word and let it speak life to you.

Keep consistently in the Word of God.
Robe yourself well from head to toe.
Live it, proclaim it,
declare it as you daily go.
Live your life immersing, dining, and feasting in it.
Stay in the Word, it will keep you out of hell.

Still I Rise

Beaten down by the cruel hands of time,
left out in the heat of the day and the cold of the night,
left to suffer and die,
unknown to many, ignored, and disrespected
by those that happen to pass by,
entrapped by hunger and poverty,
laden with burden,
stained face and tear-filled eyes, dysfunctional
but for a while.

But though roasted, toasted, confused,
and overwhelmed with the cares of life,
I did not die.
I survived.
I did not stay down.
I rise.

There were many days of sorrow,
Years of darkness, disappointments, suffering,
and pain, but nothing could hold me back.
Nothing could have kept me down.
Not forever, though dismal and impossible
it sounded and seemed.
For in my destiny it was written that I would rise.
It was written that though there would be struggles
and attempts on my life,
I would live.
I would not die.
I would rise.

So thank you, Lord, for saving me.
I am so grateful for I love and truly appreciate life.
In spite of all the challenges thrown in my path,
I thank you Lord that yet I rise to face another day
Knowing that you are in my life.

Stop Acting and Live Right

Clean up your act before it's too late.
Clean up your act and make haste.
Do the right thing, look at your life.
Look how you live, observe yourself in the light.
Get rid of the ticket stamped doom.

Stop acting and live right.
Don't waste your time living a double life.
The only one you can fool is you yourself.
Clean up your act is the best advice.
You are not too far gone to turn around and make things right.

You may think you are looking good on the stage of life.
You may be thinking you deserve an applause.
You may even be thinking of a global award.
Maybe you are proudly patting yourself on the
shoulder as an actor indeed. You are playing the part well
and you are bound to succeed.
But you'll soon find out how the wages are paid,
for the wages of sin is death and death indeed.

Stop acting and live right.
Ever since you are playing that double part
and actively dabbling in sin and its creative art,
you are slowly but surely falling apart.
You are playing the game of Russian roulette.
I beg you, my friend, play no more.
It's a game of chance and likely death.

Stop acting and live right.
It's best to throw down the balls, your guns, and all.
Clean up your act.
Play the double part no more.
Humble yourself, then relax.
Make the spiritual and necessary adjustments
to your life and acts.
Do it now.
Do it fast.

Stop Living the Ugly Life—
Life Is Too Short

Stop the cursing and the fighting.
Stop fueling hatred and malice.
Stop bickering over nothing.
Stop the lying, stealing, and cheating.
Stop the ugly living.
It's not worth it.
Life is too short.

Live not just for yourself, but live for others, too.
Live and love people, not all of them could be like you.
Be a giver and a lover.
Make this world a more attractive, gracious, and better place.

Seek to discover the good in others.
Seek to learn, understand, and appreciate the human race.
Spread all good news joyfully and enthusiastically.
Adorn the earth with your selfless beauty, finesse, and grace.
Seek to make your legacy great.
Pay attention to good living.

Color the land around you with your good deeds.
Add to it your generous portion of sweetness.
Treasure this land while living in it.
Keep it intentionally a fascinating and worthy dwelling place.
Give your life to God.

Speak to Your Mountain

Tell it to get out of your way.
Say to your mountain, "You'll stand no more."
Speak to your mountain and have no doubt.
Speak to your mountain and let it tumble down.

Speak to your mountain,
Speak out now.
Speak to your mountain,
let it crumble and fall.
Tell your mountain you are standing on God's Word.
Tell your mountain it will block you no more.

Speak to your mountain,
command it to be cast into the depth of the sea.
Speak to your mountain and command it
to disappear and live no more.
Speak to your mountain and force it to obey.
Speak to your mountain, speak out now.

Stir Up Some Fire in Me

Remove the ice cubes, they make me cold.
Take me away from the coldness I bear,
bring me into that which is closer to you.
Awaken the fire,
I want to live

Create some fire deep inside of me,
I have slept in the icebox long enough.
Now I am frozen and partially dead.
Dear Lord, light up some fire within me,
Turn on flame,
remove the coldness,
and let me begin to live.

Stretched Out

You think you are stretched beyond what you can bear.
You think you are having more than your fair share.
You think life is handing you unfair blows
and now the pain is too much for you to be quiet about,
so you tell yourself you must complain.

You are stretched out with fears, disappointments, and doubts.
Stretched out with sickness, some you would rather not talk about.
You know it.
You can feel it.
You can see it.
You can't deny it.
It's there,
but only God knows and fully understands.

Only God knows and sees the fears and tears.
Only God knows the sorrow you bear.
Only God knows and understands what it's all about.
And it's only God that can
wipe away the tears,
Relieve your pain,
And take you safely through.

Take Back What the Devil Has Stolen from You

No matter what it is that he has stolen from you,
you have the right to take it back,
regardless of what he thinks or threatens to do to you.
Take back what belongs to you.
You don't have to seek his advice nor do you have to apologize.
He is a rascal the Bible warns and advise.

He is that thief that roams all about.
Stealing and lying is his trademark.
He is a wolf in sheep's clothing.
He appears as an angel but in reality, he's the demon of death.
There is no credit for his work.
He has been stealing long enough and it's time we start taking back.
He will not willingly give up anything, so you have to put a
demand on him.
We must retrieve all from him.
We must oppose him at all cost.
We must not allow him to owe us anything.

We must be prepared to keep him bound and trampled on the ground.
We must be prepared to dethrone him.
He has stolen many things from us,
things that were all precious and dear to us.
You should not give in to him.
You should not promote his doings.
Your hope is to see him captured and punished.
Your job is to resist him
and try to live without him,
so why should he take something from us?
In fact, all He gives is misery and woe.

Nothing should we give to him.
With nothing should we allow him.
We must take back all that he has stolen from us.
We must fight against him.
We will prevail when we fight in Jesus's name.
We will prevail against him.
We will be triumphant if we trust in God.
We will be victorious through Him.
The devil is our adversary.
We will not allow him to have his way.

Take Heed, You Have Been Warned

Just to get you up to date,
just to give you Bible information, and to remind you what the
Bible says,
just so that you can't say you were not warned,
take heed.
Jesus is coming back again.

If you have been ignoring, distorting, and denying the truth,
lying to yourself and others,
Please stop and take heed to your actions and deeds
For you will not succeed and
God is not pleased
Actions taken against sin in biblical times are taking place again.
Things that happened in Bible days are happening again.
Take heed, Jesus is coming *back* again.

You have been advocating against God's Word.
You have been spreading malice, jealousy, deceit, and hate.
You have been taking your rebelliousness out on the streets.
You have been influencing and upsetting human lives.
You have been treading on dangerous ground.
Take heed to your deeds, God is displeased.
You have been warned, He's coming back again.
You will be tried for your actions and deeds.

Tear Down the Iron Curtain

Tear down the iron curtain,
let it hang no more.
Let it not block you or stand in your way.
Get away from behind it.
Get away from the bars that bind you.
Get away far from it.

Tear down the iron curtain,
get out from behind the iron fence.
Tear down the iron curtain,
it's a hindrance.

Tear down the iron curtain,
The bars that bar you in.
Tear down the iron curtain
and allow the Spirit of God to come in.

You must tear down the iron curtain
in order to expose sin.
Tear down the iron curtain that men will see
the ugly deeds of those within.
Tear down the iron curtain so that
the message of God will not be contained.
Tear down the iron curtain,
it is a distraction to the world.

Tear down the iron curtain,
Live no longer with it.
Tear down the iron curtain
and let Jesus Christ come in.

The Adversary and You

My Dearly Beloved
Just want to remind you about the adversary
that is out on the prowl.
He's armed and dangerous, roaming about,
seeking whom he may devour,
so gird up your loins.

If you are foolish or careless, he will surely
overpower and destroy you.
If, for any reason, you are lingering in the
wilderness of doubt, get out now, for
that's where he often hides out.

And now for your good and for
additional information,
I will give you a short description of him.
He wears a disguise, so don't be surprised
if he should attempt to approach you
dressed up in sheep's clothing.

When he is not in sheep's clothing, he would
like you to believe he is a roaring lion, indeed.
But, believe it or not, he is a robber,
a thief, and an accuser of the brethren in fact.
He will never be on your side
but is always quick to lie and deceive.

He's the father of lies with many children
and grandchildren. By this you should be
sick to the stomach reading his profile
and knowing that this evil one is lurking around
and is always up to some dirty old tricks,
maybe just around the corner not far from your block.

So with this knowledge, please, stay
far from him and try not to play
or hang around him
because his intention and greatest desire is to
lead you into sin.
Never try out his so-called fun and pleasure
for, to your dismay, it will not last forever.
In fact, keep yourself busy meditating
on God's Word, for the evil one has
no problem making a slave
and a fool of the unsuspecting man,
woman, boy, or girl.

He has a workshop rightly named
the devil's workshop.
He specializes in hiring idle hands,
for he pays them the wages called death
and robs them of the gift of life, and oh
how unfortunate is that?

Beloved,
In all your doing, lean unto the wisdom,
Knowledge, and understanding of God.
Don't allow the devil to have you,
or to hell, he'll take you.
He will bind you, then hit you
with a life sentence with no parole
or appeal in sight.

Take these warnings seriously
and take heed to your casual ways,
be aware and fully conscious of
the devil's works, deeds, and ways,
for it is far better
for you to be safe than sorry.
And sorry you'll be indeed.

The Author, Designer, and Finisher

He's always at work.
He leaves nothing undone.
In fact, He never stops.
He's diligent.
He authors with grace,
and designs and finishes with love and pleasure.

The author, designer, and finisher is God the Almighty
The phenomenal creator of heaven and earth.
Oh, what awesome and skillful producer and originator is He!
The master minder and maker of you and I.

The author, designer, and finisher never ceases to amaze.
He knows every one's need and supernaturally provides.
He considers not just the lilies and the birds in the trees
but all things made by His amazing and wonderful hands.

Count it your greatest blessing if you are
having a relationship with such one,
for it certainly is the greatest blessing that
man could ever have.
The author, designer, and finisher who only is God.

The Blessed Man

He walks not according to the counsel of the ungodly
Nor does he sit in the seat of the contemptuously disposed or
scornful.
But he persistently reflects and meditates on the principles,
regulations, and laws of the Almighty and Sovereign God.

He does not think of success as having wealth and fame,
But rather perceive and recognize his success as
being loaded with God's benefits, favors, and plans.
Wealth and riches are stored up in his house.
He is supernaturally provided with hidden riches from secret places.

He shall receive of the Lord royal favors.
God himself will make it possible for doors, bars of iron,
and gates of iron to be cut to let him in.
He will open unto him of His good treasure,
the heaven to give rain, and the earth to yield her increase.

He is comparable to a fruitful tree
in an amazing garden.
He is like
a refreshing spring whose water fails not,
Whose roots are forever well watered and leaves intact,
and whatsoever he does he is successful.

The blessed man shall overcome adversities
by the blood of the lamb
and the word of his testimony.
Sickness and death shall be far from him.
With long life he will be satisfied.
The Lord his God shall maintain his right, and
his effort to reach others will remain consistent with the Word.

He shall be the head and not the tail.
He shall be above and not beneath.
The Lord will rebuke the devourer for his sake.
His enemies shall fall and perish.
Nations shall be subdued on his behalf.

He shall not be afraid for the terror by night
or for the pestilence that walks at day.
His seed shall be mighty upon the earth
because he is of the generation of the righteous.
He shall not be afraid of evil tidings
because his heart is fixed trusting in the Lord.

The Book of Life

Welcome to the Book of Life.
A book that introduces and promotes eternal life.
A book that provides its readers with understanding,
love, joy, peace, and happiness.
Open it and read it to find out what is in it.
Read it, retain it, and stick to it.

Yes, the Bible is the Book of Life, the road map to Jesus Christ,
and is unlike any other book you may know.
It contains all the right answers to questions,
past, present, and future. It provides solution to everything
if you look within.
It's where the truth is laid out.
It's where true direction is given.
It encourages man to choose life
and discourages him against evil and strife.

The Bible appeals to one and all.
It surpasses race, color, and creed.
It says, "Give Jesus your life today."
Do not wait for another day.

Don't keep the Bible message to yourself.
Don't selfishly hold on to it,
share it.
Don't hide it, be sure to spread it.
Don't be quiet about it, shout it so others can hear it.

The Church

Not the one with the stained glass doors and windows,
not the one with the great pulpit
and floors covered with stainless carpet,
not the one overlooking the city,
nor the one nestling in the valley on numerous
acreage of the finest landscaped grounds.

The Church is a called-out people.
A people called and given a five-fold ministry.
A people prepared for service.
A people united in the spirit.
A people committed to live for God.

The church is not the house built for worship,
not the mass choir,
or the best known preachers that exist
but the group of people bound for the city of God.
A people with the anointed gifting.
A people led by God.

The Church will forever remain one Church.
It will forever stand.
There will be no substitute, no compromise.
It is the church of God.
It will accomplish God's plans.

The Trickster and Big Bully

The devil is a trickster and a big bully, too.
But you do not have to fear Him.
You do not have to run from him.
You do not have to hide.
Stand up to him and face him with Jesus by your side.
Declare your authority, declare war on him.

The devil is a bully and let's be fully aware of that.
According to his nature, he will always intimidate.
He's a big bully who casts his net around, seeking out
that someone that he can take facedown.
He will create chaos if you allow him.
He always has an attitude that is always foul.

His plans are cunning and worthless.
His motives are selfish and impure.
His thoughts are to harass, destroy, and to deceive.
His ultimate game plan is to own, steal from us,
kill us, or keep us bound.

The Commander of the Sea

He sees down into the deep waters.
He controls the rolling tide.
He knows all that which descend to the bottom of the ocean
to settle and to hide.
He talks to the tempest. He says, "Let love and peace abide."

He commands the sea's activities.
He performs miracles in, out, and around the shallow parts,
as well as in the deep.
He orders the sea creatures to feast, swim,
and dance in its waters.
He gives human access to fish, bathe, swim,
and take pleasure in it.

The commander of the sea sits high and look low.
He makes the sea a beauty spot in the earth,
an attraction center that will always appeal to human eyes.
He causes men to learn from it,
to discover, locate, and travel to and fro.
He never wastes time in letting
His will be done here below.

So let's pause and think how awesome
and great a commander is He to put into place
and command with such skill, love,
power, wisdom, mercy, and grace
that even the waters, the tides, and the billows
hasten to obey and perform His will and commands.

The Creator and Miracle Worker

He comes by every day.
He visits every human.
He takes trips around the globe,
yet He's never absent from our lives,
our bedsides, or our doors.

He orders every earthly thing to function
at His will.
He appoints.
He raises up.
He puts down in His own time.
He calls forth.

He dismisses,
yet never make a mistake.
He's never disappointed in the things.
He orders or creates,
for before He performs His work,
He is satisfied with the outcome.

He's the Creator and master miracle worker.
The first and the last.
The all confident.
The one and only all-powerful God.
His ability is invincible, incomparable.
We can't deny that every day we
experience Him in our lives
in some very unusual, interesting,
and supernatural way.

The Evening of Life

The morning is gone and the evening has come.
The light of day has swiftly disappeared
and the evening has come.
Night is approaching.
The friendly faces have disappeared with the day.
Beauty has faded with the dust and birds fold
their wings and refuse to sing their love songs.

Flowers and beasts are all gone from the scene,
far out of one's sight and out of one's dream.
Loved ones and families have changed their minds
and since then have claimed they have their own
matters with which to attend.

Many of the friends they once knew have
long gone ahead.
Those who have tarried are either soundly
sleeping or quietly praying.
And, sure, there are those hollering
and screaming from pain and sorrow
they have been enduring.

The evening of life has come and will surely
advance into night if the clock doesn't abruptly stop.
All seem to go silent, and then one is left all alone.
The freshness of the day is gone never to come back.
The fragrance has melted and aged away and
one must handle it the best way one can.
It's a countdown to midnight or to the place
that the clock of life stops.

The day has almost ended and the evening of life is here.
We can see the signs clearly, so why not stop whatever
you are doing and take a quick look back, give life your best shot?
Thank God for the time He has given you on this earth
and ask Him to house you in the best suite that He has got.
Give Him your heart, let Him convert it into the key,
for only through His salvation you can reserve a heavenly spot.

The Eyes of God

Nothing escapes the eyes of God.
His eyes are in every place.
It spans the world up and down.
He watches over everything.

The tiniest object that falls to the ground.
The largest creature that crawls around.
God moves His eye to and fro.
He concerns Himself with every detail,
whether in the dark or in the light.

He never slumbers, He never sleeps,
but gives perfect attention to all His inventions.
He masters His duty using His eyes.
Nothing slips from His eyesight.
Nothing escapes His radar.
Nothing, no matter how near or far.

God has smart eyes, and with His eyes He captures all.
He sees the hurting families.
He sees the orphan girls and boys.
He sees the old, as well as the young.
His eyes is on the baby lamb,
no matter how far it strays or runs.

The Finger of God

How busy, how accurate, how powerful,
how impressive it is,
calling man away from sin
and back to Him.

The finger of God,
Like an arrow, it points.
Like a compass, it directs.
Like a clock, it shows and tells,
pointing out and showing man what
is right and what is wrong.

Let the finger of God
be an arrow to you.
Let it be a compass to direct you,
and the clock that will show
and tell you what time is it,
for time is later than you think.

The Garden of Eden

God gave this garden to Adam and Eve
To be their home and dwelling place,
To be the place where they could multiply and increase,
To be the perfect place where He could meet with them
face-to-face.
There were flowers and fruit-bearing trees,
decorating every space on the ground.
There must have been fishes and fowls, birds, beasts, and butterflies
gleefully, delightfully, and leisurely chirping,
fluttering, dancing, roaming, and floating about.
Oh, yes, it happened in this wonderful garden, the garden of Eden.
A friendly, warm, and comforting place.
A place where nothing was lacking.

The beautiful garden, the one called Eden, the one read about.
The garden where creation took place.
The garden where humanity began.
A place where cool, sparkling rushing water could be found.
A place where herbs and vegetables abound.
A place free from walls and iron gates.
A place where one could safely walk about.
A cool and relaxing garden with no doubt.

The garden of Eden, for that was its name.
A garden with much history attached, a garden we shouldn't forget.
But this is the garden where sin came to be known.
An act that time cannot erase.
For when the serpent with a deceptive intention
chose to look in Eve's face concocted a story and told her a lie.

She listened to his fable and got caught up in it.
She became overwhelmed and abided by it.
She then got her husband to join in the act.
Their performance created confusion
and soon became known as the sin of disobedience.
They were indicted and found guilty of a crime.
Together they were charged as partners in crime
and ultimately were axed from the garden,
the beautiful garden of Eden.

The garden of Eden will not be forgotten,
although it may be remembered as the first crime scene.
But thanks to God the Almighty, an appeal was granted,
and instead of life sentence, man has been pardoned
and granted a reprieve.
We can all celebrate. We should all be thankful to God that
He chose to redeem us by the blood of the precious lamb.

The Heathen Rage

The heat is on in our land
And the heathen have their cruel and ungodly plans.
Yes, their rage is on and they are in utter confusion.
They imagine wicked, miserable, and vain things.
They mock, jeer, and persecute our God
and wallow hopelessly in their sins.

They dare to hassle and persecute those who speak nobly in
honoring Him.
They will not stop.
They are relentless in their efforts and attacks.
The stench is overwhelming.
But wait, our God will speak.
Surely, He will bring justice and peace in time.
His judgment promised to be quick, harsh, powerful but just.

So let the heathen rail, rant, and rage.
Let them continue to imagine vain things.
Let them continue to do their thing.
But let them not look for mercy when judgment comes.
For then it might be a bit too late to try to obtain an escape.

The Hero and Supreme God

The one who creates signs and wonders.
The one who is able to rise above all circumstances
make the difficult to become simple
wins battles and never loses one.

Let me tell you about Him.
How He championed human causes,
laid down His life for all people,
and how he raised Himself up
so that we may live.

When you come to know Him, then
you will understand why He is the only
hero and supreme God that man could ever have.

The Hope within Lives On

It grows, it never stops,
it points to new, better, and exciting days ahead.
It foretells a bright future and changes in
circumstances regarding plans.
It looks up to the sky in the heaven.
It encourages the sun to rise and shine
and casts its great light over the earth.

The hope within lives on.
It never gives up.
It holds on to the hands of the hopeless.
It takes them to places blessed, beautiful, and serene.
It dreams, it sings.
It declares things wonderful.

It is never weary.
It is never worn.
It remains bold, it remains calm, it remains strong.
It always plans,
ready and prepared to conquer.

It is an overcomer.
It speaks success.
It speaks happiness.
It gently but sweetly pronounces the future.
It leans on the Word for revelation.
It's a comforter.
The hope within lives on beyond tomorrow.

The Hopeless Man

He dwells in a world of his own,
a world called hopeless world,
a godless world.
He lives on the street of hopelessness
and dines and feasts with the hopeless
at the table of hopelessness.

He wallows in self-pity
And bathes in the stream of bitterness.
He murmurs and complains.
He wears the badge of hopelessness
and embraces doom and gloom.
He speaks the language of hopelessness
and confesses his hopeless destiny.
He hangs on to hopelessness
and calls it his very own.

He drinks the wine of forgetfulness
and get intoxicated on hopelessness.
The hopeless man spends his days living in fear,
his years living in despair, and his nights
having nightmares.
He has no hope in anything.
He plays the blame game and, according
to him, He is life's victim.

The Intruder—He Came Right In

He did not knock., he pushed his way in.
He entered and disrupted everything.
He made no calls before he came.
He just came bursting in through the doors.
He did not seem embarrassed at all.
He came in and wanted control of everything.

I had to let him know his place,
and let him know that his behavior I would not tolerate.
But when I began to study the Word and pray,
he began to shake, hide his face, and back away.
I kept the momentum up.
I would not allow him any space.
I sure wanted him to make a hasty retreat.
I really wanted him out of my place.

I have seen him acting like this before
I have observed him making his way into many people's doors.
I have myself experienced him before.
In fact, I was under his counsel for many years
and was sadly deceived by him all those days, weeks, and months.
He is a deceiver, of course, so what do you think?
I told him he has been around too long to be unknown.
I did not want another moment entertaining
him in my life or my home.
I had to get him out of my space and life.

He is what he is.
He seeks no permission to enter into your place.
He will always try, but if you are vigilant and wise,
you can rest assured that he will not be able to get
you out of the race or seize your space.

The Lord Is My Shepherd

The Lord is my shepherd, He watches over me.
In places of barrenness, He never will lead me.
I shall not lack for anything, for
He is with resources filled.
He will turn my darkness into light
and give me great insights to what's right.
And take me to higher heights.

He gives me a place to lay my head
and a garment of praise to go to bed.
He provides me with my every meal
and instructs me how to take my feed.
He instructs me in the path to go
and make me feel safe and at ease.
I have no need to doubt Him.

Besides still waters, He leads me
and to refreshing springs He guides me.
I have no need to fear a foe,
although in shadowy places I sometimes go.
He prepares a table filled for me
and feeds me in the presence of my enemies.

He restores my soul.
He makes me whole.
And though I walk in the valley of death,
death shall not overpower me.
I fear no evil night or day,
for my shepherd is beside me all the way.

The Man on the Inside

That's the inner man.
That's the man with the authority.
The honored man,
the sobered man, the wise man,
the man that better understands.

Thank God for the man,
That just, sincere, and true man.
The man that awakens one's
conscience and gives rise to clear,
clean thoughts.
The man that points us
to the true light even in the
middle of the darkest night.

The man on the inside is the inner man.
He is the man that reasons and coaches
and gives us sobering advice.
He is never rude or pushy,
Never overbearing or loud.
This man on the inside is the
best man in our lives.

The Midnight Call

The script has been written.
The stage has been set.
The main players have taken their respective places.
The curtains will be pulled back any time now
and the drama will begin.
But are you ready and prepared for it?

This will be the greatest act the world will ever experience,
the greatest presentation that will ever happen.
It will be the day of the mighty hour of the midnight call.
All will be involved some way, somehow or another.

The scenes will unfold rapidly, swifter than you can think,
faster than lightning flashes, and smoother than you can wink.
No hitching, no actor will be found missing or fail to act.
And don't you dare think for even a moment that
you'll not be an actor in the plot.

It will be the mighty disappearance of those who dare to believe and
trust God.
There will be weeping and wailing because many of our loved ones will
take a flight without looking back, leaving friends and families behind,
many of whom will be caught off guard because it could happen in
the middle of the night when they least expect it and they are living
their usual life.
But none will be able to say they were not warned or advised.

The midnight call could come any time now, for it's later than you think.

The midnight call should not be ignored or neglected because as night follows day many will live in regret, many will be disappointed, and many tears will fall but many will rejoice that they have answered the heavenly call.

The Miracle Worker

The miracle worker is out every day,
Impacting and changing lives every minute of the day.
If you need a miracle, you'll need to check with Him.
His mercies are multiplied and His compassion fails not.
He is never too busy to speak a word of comfort or to act.

This miracle worker cannot be stopped.
His phenomenal and unmatched power is amazing.
He's never intimidated by number or size,
just reach out to Him as He passes by.
He's attracted to human cries.

This miraculous business of His began at a wedding
and up until now it is still flourishing.
He's the miracle worker of yesterday, today, and forever.
A miracle worker who transcends time, reason, and space.
He's the miracle worker who never stumbles, grumbles,
disappoints, or makes mistakes.

He resurrects, He appoints,
He calls forth,
He dismisses,
He rises up,
He takes down at His will and orders even storms to stand still.
The miracle worker and creator is the man Jesus Christ.

Then They Came to the Red Sea

Years of harassment,
Years of bondage,
Slavery, and embarrassment,
then Pharaoh decided to let the
Israelite people go.

Stick, straws, and bricks did
not break their bones,
but wilderness life made them trembled,
complained, and cried.

In Egypt with leeks and onions
they were fed.
In the wilderness, fresh manna God sent them instead.
But nothing He did made them content.
They chose to blame Moses for almost
everything he did or said
When they finally left Egypt, Pharaoh
and his host soon decided
to pursue them,
for he thought he should overtake,
overpower, and destroy them.

And so, to the road of destruction he ignorantly took.
And thus, the momentum begins
and the drama unfolded and increased.
But wait with me until at the edge of
the Red Sea they reached.

The Israelite people saw the deep,
frightening waters before them.
And as Pharaoh and his host closely
followed behind them, they panicked.
They shook in their boots.
You should have been there to see them.

They wailed, they screamed,
they yelled and hollered indeed.
They wished they had stayed behind.
They wished they had not fled
the Egyptian scene.
For now, they were soon to be caught up with.
They felt deceived.
They felt foolishly trapped.
And it was all Moses's fault, they decided.

Pharaoh sped up his chariot.
His army followed,
They were ready and anxious to shed
the Israelite's blood.
They were prepared for the nastiest fight.
They were ready to take lives.

Then God whispered to Moses
to stretch forth his rod over the Red Sea.
And as he did so and quicker than
lightning could flash, the sea parted.
And as if out from nowhere,
a clear walking path appeared before them.

The Israelite people did not hesitate.
They stepped forward and before long
they were all safe on the other side of the
Red sea, just in time to see Pharaoh
and his host stepping in in haste and in glee.
But the parted waters quickly retook its
shape and its place,
And Oh!

The waters of the Red sea came down in haste,
overpowered, overthrew, and welcomed them
to a watery grave.
And sure enough, the last I heard of them,
they are still lying dead at the bottom
of the Red Sea.

The Reality of Life

When you are down in the mud, few, if any, will want to get you out.
When you are on top of the world, all will want to join
you dancing with the stars.
When you have money, the world will gladly embrace
and spend it with you.
When you are broke, they will take off into space.

If you are happy and singing a great song, many will
gladly sing along while holding your hands.
But if, for any reason you all hit the wrong note,
be not surprised the error is only on you, and as sure
as night follows day, you are the one that caused
them to mess up the note.

Woe to you, my brother, if grief you encounter.
Woe to you, my sister, if for long it lingers.
Friends like those of Job will only blame you.
Don't expect them to stay around with you,
for they will quickly move on.
Because in the reality of life,
those who seem closest to you may be the real devils posing
as real Christians.

The Road I Travel

It's not always easy or smooth.
It has its bumps, valleys, hills, and mountains.
It has its runs, it has its crawls,
it has its ups and downs.
Yet it is a road that I, like many others, must travel—
a road that is sometimes dark and slippery.
A road marked with pain and sorrows, disappointments,
Failures, and many other challenges.
But though uncertain, there's hope for a better tomorrow,
and it's better to live in hope than in despair.

The road I travel sometimes seem broad, sometimes
narrow, winding, and tiresome, and unpaved in many parts.
It would appear sometimes very lonely, although there
are many other travelers there. The road I travel
holds a mystery, you know when you get on
but you can't be sure when and where you will get off.

The road I travel is called life and is traveled by all alive.
It is a road we all must travel, as long as we are in this life.
It's a road that offers different experiences and perspectives.
A road that is sometimes long and dreary, short and sweet.
Whatever it may be, it's a road we cannot avoid.
But often many times, it's said to be too short.

The Season of Change Has Come

Let the barren bring forth.
The wailing women weep no more,
but sing aloud and dance unto the Lord their God and King.
Let the poor, the lame, the weak, the needy,
and the destitute be delivered and be made full.
For the season of change has come.

The season of change has come.
It is upon us
and we are seeing the light of a new day.
The glory cloud is hanging over us.
Thank God for this new and wonderful day.
Thank God I am part of it.
It is a great day.

Let the widows and the orphans begin
to sing a new song.
Let them begin to rejoice, for the
showers of blessings are at hand.
Let the earth be wet with the dew
and the blessings of heaven.
This is a new season.
Let us rejoice and be glad.

This is a new day and God's people are in it.
It's a glorious season and I can feel it
The season of change has come and we are walking in it.
The darkness has faded.
Lack has vanished and suddenly there
is a burst of abundance.
It's a good feeling.
Glory to God, I am enjoying it.

The Set Time Is Now

It's a season of blessings.
A time of refreshing.
A glorious time of reaping and taking
back that which was stolen or lost.
That time is now.

The devourer came in and robbed you,
but now a double portion awaits.
Caterpillar and palmer and canker worm,
no more from me you'll steal anymore.
I close down your entryway, I cut off your supply.
Now is my time to rejoice

The Sound of Rain

I can hear the pitter-patter on the roof.
I can see the dark clouds shifting
and allowing the rain to take its place.
And now I can hear the sound of rain
as an abundance comes pounding on
the rooftop and on my windowpane.

Yes, I can see the rain.
I can hear the sound.
And there's a pitter-patter on the outside
and above my head.
It's an abundance, I am glad.

For long we have endured the drought.
God is taking action now.
He's blessing.
He's rewarding.
He's stomping the drought out.
He's answering to the rain seekers.
He's telling them He has heard their prayers.
He's supplying with an abundance.
He's supplying the rain.

I can hear it.
I can see it.
It's appealing.
It's refreshing.
Souls are responding to it.
It's not the ordinary but the extraordinary.
It's not the usual but the unusual.
It's not the natural but the supernatural.
It's the sound of rain.

The Spy in the Sky

Make no mistake, there's a spy in the sky
looking out for you and I.
He has eyes that are clear, sharp, and precise.
Check out His work,
He is an expert.
He sees everything.
He uncovers hidden things.

He is the spy of all spies,
always looking out for His people from the skies.
There are those who selfishly and foolishly claim
He's there to sneak on mankind.
Some who think He is there to make swift
and tough demands on their lives.
Some others think He is there with eyes and hands
that are strict, swift, and severe.
While some think it doesn't matter to Him even if we fail.
But until we know He loves and cares for us,
until we know and fully understand, acknowledge,
and come to appreciate,
He is our only reliable and trustworthy watchman
and authority, looking out for us here and from the sky.

The Steps of a Good Man

They are ordered by God.
They don't just happen.
They are planned and purposed.
With careful, courageous, and impressive hands,
He carved out everyone.

He doesn't allow mistakes to happen.
He's exemplary and perfect in all His ways.
He wants man to walk in His footstep,
so He mapped out and colored the way.

The steps of a good man, they are ordered
to help him on life's way.
And though at times the journey is hazardous,
God always has a way.

The Unrestrained Barking Dog

He sets himself to bark at everything in sight.
He doesn't care if it's day or night.
He grumbles, he growls, he howls.
He has no peace at all.
He must be restrained.
He should not be allowed to disturb
the peace of the town.

He must be restrained.
He should be shut down.
He sends out false alarms.
He keeps the babies awake.
He scares visitors away.
He sets things in disarray.
He makes a nuisance of himself.
He is the alarm that keeps you tense.
He is the unrestrained barking dog
that creates havoc in the town.

The Whisper in the Wind

There's a whisper in the wind.
There's a message it brings,
A message of hope refreshing and glorious blessings.
There's a whisper in the wind,
so let's quietly listen in.

For on a day such as this,
the sun closes its eyes,
the moon covers its face,
the darkness then descends and takes its place.
Then it lingers to allow a wind to pass through,
followed by a crackling cry from the woods nearby
and a whisper in the wind.

It's like a musical melody and a cheer to my ears.
It creates a marvel on the land and in the trees.
The earth smiles, stand at attention.
The trees bop their heads
while their branches choose to wave their
leafy fingers, and hands crackling
and dancing as if they are glad.
And, as if out of nowhere the whisper appears.
A whisper in the wind.

The whisper in the wind, the one that I hear.
A whisper that tells me that God is working
wonders even among the trees.
A whisper so sweet,
it's a solemn affair.
A whisper so unique and sweet,
it makes the birds sleep.

The Word of God

The Word of God is life.
I must keep it in my heart.
I must keep it in my mouth.
I must meditate on it day and night.
From it, I must never depart.

The Word of God gives life.
It is my daily bread.
It is powerful, quick, and sharp.
It will not fail its mark.
It's the arrow that pierces human's heart.

The Word of God is designed to meet all needs.
It is man's greatest supplier.
If you say you want a better life,
If you say you love Jesus Christ,
Seek out the Word for your desires.
Seek the Word for the best advice.

Think on These Things

There is so much to ponder,
So much to talk about,
So much to think and wonder,
So much that the world would like us to worry about.
But let this mind be in you—the mind of Christ.

Be encouraged.
Be enabled to
think godly,
think wisely,
think soberly,
think optimistically and favorably, and remove all doubts.

Think on these things:
things that are honest,
things that are just,
things that are pure,
things that are lovely,
things that are of good report.
If there be any virtue, if there be any praise, think
steadfastly on these things.

This Is Your Time

Step out into it,
The delays are over.
God is about to show up on your behalf.
This is your time, come walk in it.
This is your time, don't let it slip.
Make good use of it.

This is your time, your time to crossover.
Your time for the overflow,
Make room for it.
Get up and get to it.
This is your time to activate, achieve, and receive.
Get up and get to it.
This is your moment arranged by God.
This is the time to capture it.

This Life of Mine

This life of mine, I sometimes find it difficult.
Yet I can't deny that
most of the time it is very interesting
and rather amazing.
This is the life God gave to me.
I try to live it as I should.
It is by faith I live it.

I wake up in the mornings not
knowing what transpired while I slept.
I know it's God that kept me through the
long, lonely nights, but pop my eyes open
at morning light so that I could climb
out of bed to fellowship with Him
and keep up with the day ahead.

This life of mine,
I give it back to the Lord.
It is He that keeps my heart
beating and my blood rightly flowing.
And sure, now and then,
He visits me with dreams and visions.

This life of mine,
The life God gave to me,
I call it precious.
I call it sweet.
I call it interesting and amazing.
My desire is to honor God in all of it.

Tomorrow I Do Not Have

I make no plans for tomorrow.
It is not promised to me.
It may not come.
I may never see it.
For in reality, it does not exist.

Tomorrow, I do not have.
I make no provision for it.
I make no joke about it.
I welcome and embrace each
day as it comes along and
gladly call it today.

For tomorrow I will not hope or pray.
I will not disappoint myself,
knowing I will not have it.
I will live for today and be
satisfied with it.

Turn On the Music

Turn on the music,
Let it play loud and sweet.
Turn on the music,
Let it speak.

Too many souls are burdened,
Too many are sad,
Too many are crying because they are cast down.
Too many have not heard it and not looking out.

Let the music play on,
Let's listen to it attentively.
Let's listen to the lyrics, the rhythm, and the sound.
There is a melody, a message, and comfort in it.
Let's listen intentionally to what's coming out.

Hope rises from its lyrics.
Hope rises from its sound.
It flutters like a butterfly.
It reaches out, it whispers, it shouts.

Turn on the music,
Keep it playing long.
Turn it to its maximum,
it will create a stir.
let it soothe, let it inspire,
let it heal, let it deliver,
let the saddened be comforted.
Let the weak, lonely, and cast down
listen to the music and rise to their feet.

Two Roads—Which Will You Take?

There are two roads before you, which will you take?
Two roads before you, each leading a different way.
Two roads, one going to the left the other to the right.
Two roads before you, one broad and wide, the other narrow and straight,
Which will you take?

The road on the left is overly traveled.
It's built to attract pleasure-seekers, money hunters, the so-called
powerful and the elites.
The road on the right is narrow and straight, yet is built to
accommodate the humble and all those who will faithfully follow. It's a
sacred walk and only the faithful God chasers will stay on its path.

There are two roads before you, but only one you can travel.
Two roads before you, which will you follow or take?
The broad on the left or the narrow on the right?
Two roads before you, which will you take?
The crowded, paved, and glamorous or the hard, the straight,
and glorious.
Two roads before you, which will you take?

Two roads before you, which will you take?
Two roads before you, each leading to a direct but different place.
Two roads before you, which will you take?
The one that leads to a fiery place
or the one that leads into the pearly gates.
Two roads before you, it's up to you to choose one.
Two roads before you, which will you take?
Make no mistake.
There are two roads before you,
Which will you take?

We Fan the Flame

We fan the flame of evil.
Oh yes, we do.
We embrace things that are ugly and untrue.
We strive for man's anointing.
We boast in our achievements and accomplishments.
We idolize fame and fortune.
We silently and secretly undermine and compromise.
We become haters of righteousness and lovers of political correctness.
We favor those who think like us but disfavor those who dare to differ.
We murmur, yell, curse, and swear when rebuked regarding wrongs.
We pick up our knives and guns, then stab and shoot.
We pronounce death and destruction upon those
who do not walk, talk, or act like us.
We hail the sun, moon, and stars, but reject
and deny the Creator of them all.
Oh yes, we fan the flame of evil and wrongs.

We Wait until He Comes Back

We wait for Him.
We, the sons and daughters of Zion.
We wait here under an open heaven
and a sun blazing sky.
We wait until He comes.

We wait in patience.
We wait with bated breath.
We wait with watchful eyes.
We strive to rescue the neglected,
the broken, and the lost.
We seize and embrace each
moment that we wait.

While we wait, we will not ignore
or neglect the importance of the culture
or the time in which we are living.
We will not fail to redeem it.
While we wait, we must confront evil.
We must reach out our hands and hearts to those
who do not know Jesus Christ as Lord.

We must refuse to sit idly while evil flourish
and people die like flies, wickedness
takes on prominence, invades our streets, declare war,
and take on new wings and fly.
We must refuse to compromise
or associate ourselves with wrongs.

We must refuse to live ungodly and lawless lives.
We must refuse to imitate, echo,
or embrace that which does not bring honor
and glory to the king of Kings and the Lord of lords.

We must refuse to speak the language
or cry the cry of the feeble, the wicked,
and the ungodly man.
We must refuse to join the ranks of the maddening crowd.
Instead, we must desire to live not for ourselves
but only for the King.

If we be sons and daughters of Zion,
we must separate ourselves unto righteousness.
We must be on the lookout.
We must be on our knees.
We must stay in line.
We must be fully equipped, dressed,
ready and waiting, and
always abiding in the Word.

I therefore charge you, O sons
and daughters of Zion,
let your lights shine brightly.

Let it shine gloriously,
Proclaiming the gospel truth,
upholding His wonderful name,
and be prepared to lay down even your lives.
This is the message. This is for you as you wait
until He comes back.

Wailing Women

Wail, weep, cry aloud, plead, beg, and ask.
Reach out to God on bended knees,
Touch Him with your words,
hands, hearts, and deeds.
Cry like a woman who has
lost her only child,
cry out as one in deep distress.

Take up the cause, rise up, and cry.
Weep, women, weep and wail for the lost.
Cry out as one who is wounded
and is about to lose one's life.
Travail and sigh as one in deep heartfelt pain.
Call out to God in fervent prayer.
Let your wailing be seen and heard.
Weep, wail, and cry, women, there is a cause.

Cry as one in great need of help.
Cry as one needed to be rescued.
Cry as one desperate for life.
Abandon yourself and wail as one giving birth.
Plead your cause, cry as one in deep fear and sorrow.
Cry with groaning and in pain.
Reach out, wailing women, and bring
in the destitute, wounded, and the lost.

Wait on God

Wait on Him.
Whatever He says to do, do it.
It doesn't matter how long it takes, wait!
It may seem hard to do,
but those who have waited before
have been given reason to rejoice.
Join the list of those who have benefited by
waiting on Him.

Take comfort and don't give up,
Just wait patiently for Him.
He will never be late.
He may come at the time
you least expect Him.
Wait on Him.

We Wrestle

We wrestle not against human, tigers, or bears.
We wrestle not against the things we may
touch, see, or hear.
But we wrestle against spiritual forces
in the atmosphere.

Put your full armor on, children.
Be covered from head to toe.
The fight is on, the battle is real.
Darts and arrows are being hurled
everywhere.
Evil and wicked forces are out on the
prowl, wrestling with humans
wherever they are found.

So be not ignorant.
Be ready and well prepared.
Wrestle not inadvisably or fearful,
But confidently, diligently, trusting always
in the Word of God.
Remember that we wrestle not against
the things and people of this world
but against forces stronger and more
powerful than the physical man.
So put your spiritual armor on,
have your protective gears in hand.

To triumph in this battle, stay on the Lord's side.
Follow the Word.
Be spiritually, mentally, and physically
ready and prepared at all times.

What Do You Do?

What do you do when it seems as if your expectations have crashed
against the rocks of despair?
What do you do when it seems God is not operating as His words
indicate?
What do you do when it seems that God has changed His mind
concerning you?
Tell me, what do you do when the things you have been claiming
by faith have been eluding you?
Isn't it a fact that there are times when it would appear as if God has
forgotten you?
Isn't it a fact that there are times when it seems that He is taking
back the blessings that He has given to you?
Isn't it a fact that there are times when you think He is deliberately
punishing you?
So what do you do?
How do you feel about the times that you expect Him to show up
and He does not?
Do you wonder where He was or why He did not show up?
Do you wonder if He has really forgotten you?
Is it that you may have missed the mark and the devil has been
given all the power over you?
Sometimes we allow ourselves all of the above, but the thing to do
is not let your feelings get the better of you, just abide in Him, He'll
always be true.
He will always come through for you.

What If He Didn't?

He thought about me from the beginning of time.
He thought about me.
He kept me on His mind.
He knew the steps I would take.
He knew the mistakes I would make.
He knew that the adversary would come after me.
He knew the victim I would be.
He thought about me and He made a way for my escape.
But what if He didn't?

What if, for me, He didn't die on the cross?
What if, for me, He didn't pay the ransom cost?
What if, for me, He didn't rise from the dead?
What if He didn't love and care for me?
I wouldn't be free.
I would be lost.
I would be dead.
I would be bound for hell.

What's Happening in Our Land?

Another day of trauma,
Another day of hell at school,
Another day filled with sorrow,
Another day of fatality,
Another day of separating the
wounded and the living from the dead.
That's what I heard the reporter said.

They huddled and bundled into closest spaces.
They found themselves hiding under
tables, benches, and chairs.
They felt trapped, they were fearful.
They were in utter shock.
They could hear clearly the noise of the flying bullets.
By then, they knew quite well some angry,
heartless person was trying to destroy them.
He wanted to see them dead.

This was not a movie in action.
It was a live scene, another occurrence that
emphasizes that we are not
safe anywhere, not even in our homes,
churches, or in our schools.
What is this happening with our people in
our land.? Is the world gone angry or totally mad?

Things have become traumatic,
ugly, horrible, horrific, and sad.
Bad news mark our headline news almost every day.
When will we hear some good news? I ask and pray.
When will we seek God in a special way?
Isn't it time we realize that something has gone wrong?
And isn't it time we realize we need God in our land?
What is happening with our people?
Is it that many have gone mad?
Only God knows and understands.

And I sigh in pain, open my mouth, and said,
"Oh God, cover us with your Almighty hands.
Please guide and protect your people wherever
they are throughout this land."

What Manner of Man Is This?

What manner of man is this
who claims that He is the Son of God
who actually allowed Himself to be nailed to a cross?
What manner of man is this
that went about doing only good?
He raised the dead,
healed the sick,
calmed storms,
fed five thousand,
raised Himself from the dead.
What manner of man is this?

What manner of man is this?
Persecuted, ridiculed, rejected, bruised for human cause,
yet He opened not His mouth.
The most controversial, mysterious figure
who ever lived who ever died, who ever rose from the dead,
Seen by thousands.
What manner of man is this?
He is the son of the Almighty God.

What Part Are You Playing as a Christian?

Some Christians love to go on foreign missions.
Some love to locally evangelize.
Some love to preach and teach the Word.
Some love to sing in the church choir.
Some love to make financial contributions.
Some love to fast, watch, and pray.
But what part do you play?

Are you actively building God's kingdom
or are you building your own kingdom here on earth?
Are you involved in spreading the Gospel of Jesus Christ
or are you attached to the gossips and the brawls and fake news?
Are you willingly tithing
or are you there to condemn and criticize every financial action?

Are you praying for your church sisters and brothers
or are you the one ready to throw them into hell?
It's unfortunate that there are Christians operating against
the teachings of the Bible, and therefore missing the mark.
And if that's you, it's time to get out and away from the dark.

When Christians Get Involved

When Christians get involved, see what happens.
There's sure to be a marked difference.
The atmosphere is changed.
Expect positive outcome,
Expect to see the hands of God extended,
Then watch things work out for your good.

God will not fail to use Christians
to demonstrate His involvement,
show His greatness and His love.
He will always show up.
He will perform.
He will give the right answer.
He will always have His way.

He will work wonders like those that we read about,
even when we can't see them with our naked eyes
and sometimes have our doubts that they will work out.
When Christians get involved, God will always intervene.
He will always make things worthwhile, good, and wonderful.

When Darkness Falls

You don't have to be told how vulnerable one can be
when the sun turns its face and darkness takes its place.
When darkness falls, many there be
that think it's time to go wild
or relax and reflect on what they have done
up until the end of the day (for the day).

When darkness falls, some are left to fend for themselves,
holler, howl, and weep, get into bed, and sleep
or go out into the town, act like a smart and decent human
or a fool and a clown.
When darkness falls, things happen, my friend,
some you just can't stop to imagine or think.

I hate to tell you that darkness is an opportunist
that attracts and invites trouble.
It embraces and encourages sorrow and wrongs.
It provides arms, legs, covering, and support,
and in aid of robbery, abuse, and assaults.
For when darkness falls the enemy prowls around looking
and seeking for whom he may assault or devour in the dark.

When darkness falls, it's no time to fool around
But a time to kneel down and fill the earth with a joyful sound.
A time to stop the enemy from making attacks and prowling around.
When darkness falls, be sure, my friend, to be one of those
that will call out to God for divine protection for man.

When in Search

As you go searching for treasures,
treasures that are precious, rare, and hard to find,
you should first think of Jesus because
He is the greatest treasure
one could ever seek to find.

As you go searching for answers,
Good answers, great answers, right answers,
you must look to Jesus, He has all the answers
no matter the question you ask.

When you go looking for friendship,
look to Jesus. He's the best friend
one could ever seek to find.
He'll never disclose your secret.
He'll comfort, guide, and protect you
and will always be at hand to help you.

When You Trust in God

You shall never be ashamed.
When you trust in God, expect
your life to change.
When you trust in God, you can expect
good things to happen.
When you trust in God, you can shout
hallelujah as if you're on
your way to heaven.

God is a covenant-keeping God.
He keeps His covenant to
a thousand generation.
Those that trust in Him
is destined to win.
You, too, can be a winner if you
would only trust Him.

Where Are They Now?

They are gone.
People I came to know
and grew up to appreciate and to love.
Many were seniors.
They were either my parents' neighbors or friends.
But where are they now?
They have moved on.
They are gone.
They are dead.

Some left us heartbroken and saddened.
They were good people.
Some were fun people.
But some left us wounded with the trouble they made.
Some left us more certain we won't see them ever again.

Where are they now? I must contemplate.
They all went on a journey and did not return.
Where are they now after not saying goodbye?
The people we grew up to know.
The people who helped to raise us right.
The people who put themselves into our lives.
The people who corrected us as our parents often do.
Where are they now?
They are gone out of sight.
Gone from our lives.

Who Art Thou, Goliath?

Who art thou, O Goliath, that I should be afraid?
You may boast of all your strength, adventures,
and conquests but I will not be intimidated
or be afraid of you, uncircumcised Philistine.

You may rehearse your many stories,
declare your resume,
Say them loud and clear.
Tell the world that you are the greatest warrior,
and yet I will not care or fear.

I will not be your victim
but I will see to your end.
The fowls of the air and the beasts of the field,
your body they will tear and share.

Who art thou, O Goliath?
To your words I will not adhere.
You claim to be a champion and a warrior,
but the greatest champion is on my side
and shall destroy and annul your
so-called fame and name.

Who art thou, O Goliath?
You claim to be a giant.
You claim to be a champion.
But I also perceive you as a boaster,
a deceiver, a loser, and a liar.
And in the name of God the Almighty,
I shall cut you down this hour.

Who but God Doeth All Things Well?

Who but God could dress the heaven so beautifully,
so gloriously, magnificently, and so wonderfully?
Who but God could permit the moon
and stars to shine so bright at nights?
Who but God could fitly order all things
into organized and perfect space?
Who but God could cause the earth
to bud and to increase?
It's for you to think and ask.
Who but God could do such marvelous
and amazing things?

Who but God doeth all things well?
The heaven to stand in its place and the
earth to sit below.
The heaven to be draped with patterns of clouds
and the earth to reflect all that is in it.
Who but God decorates the earth
and let man call it his abiding place?
Who but God?

Who but God tells the heaven to send down rain,
robed alongside it a rainbow, create a thunderous sound,
and let lightning flash to accompany it?
Who but God could cause the earth to show
forth His handiwork
and the heaven to declare and display His glory?
Who but God is in all of this?
Please tell me.
Who else could it be but God?

With All My Heart

I will search for Him until I find Him,
He whom my soul longs and thirsts for.
I will not rest or be satisfied until I find Him.
I will spend the time looking for Him.

With all my heart I want to know Him.
With all my heart I desire Him.
I want to drink from His cup.
I want to share in His sufferings.

Jesus, I want to get closer to you.
I want to get involved in your business
and to work alongside of you,
hang around with you.

I want you to know that I love you.
I want to touch your wounded side.
I want to see the nail prints in your hands and feet.
Master, with all my heart I want to love you.

With All That's Been Said and Done

Good people have spoken, given good advice,
yet with all that's been said and done,
we are still locked in foolish fights.
Lives have been sacrificed.
Families have been torn apart.
Tears have been shed.
Positions lost and opportunities denied.
We blame everybody except ourselves.

We make speeches that hatch out the grave
spot and seal the tomb.
Vicious despicable attacks on one another.
We rehearse and foolishly declare
negative thoughts and feelings over our lives.
We have heard of and seen far too many deadly hours,
far too many horrific moments,
far too many murdered lives,
far too many eulogies read,
far too many times we are forced to say,
"Goodbye and rest in peace,"
as unfathomable tragedies seem
to become the new norm.

We borrow from Martin Luther King's remarks.
We quote Rodney King's words, too.
But in reality, can't we not get along?
We make many statements,
yet with all we say and do, lives are being taken,
lives are being lost.
It's heart-wrenching.
How many more times are we willing
to hear the words alarming, troubling,
hostile, shocking, lawless before we stop
playing the fool?
Are we satisfied or we confused?

Who Can Put Humpty Together Again?

Fallen into the pit of despondency,
sunken in the mire,
wounded and broken from top to bottom,
covered with grief, covered with shame,
Humpty has slipped, Humpty has fallen,
Humpty has failed.

Now she needs a makeover
And a start over, too.
She needs a godly repair.
She needs to be born again.

Who can put Humpty together again?
Who can provide the repair?
Humpty might have been a dear relative or friend,
but when pride took over
and sin knocked her over,
she tumbled, staggered, and hit the ground.

If, like Humpty, you have slipped, fallen,
and failed to look to Jesus.
He can put you back together again.

When the Bridegroom Came

The fools were asleep.
They had no oil in their lamps.
They were not ready for the wedding feast.

When the bridegroom came,
the wise were ready and waiting.
Their lamps were filled with oil
and the burners burning bright
and they were well prepared to enter the feast.

The bridegroom will not tarry when He gets to your door.
He is coming expecting you to be ready to go with Him.
He's coming, expecting you to join Him for the feast.
He will not come begging, beseeching,
or forcing you to attend the wedding.
But will gladly take you with Him if
you are ready and waiting for Him.

He will reject and refuse the foolish and the slothful,
the unprepared and the neglectful,
but will gladly take with Him the wise
and the careful, the prepared and the diligent.
They will participate in the great marriage feast to come.

While I Live

Let me live in peace, giving respect and receiving respect.
Let me not be dependent on government or anyone to provide me
with the resources I am capable of providing for myself.
Let me strive to do all that I can to make this world a better place.
Let me think soberly and objectively,
even in the face of adversities and disappointments.
Let me live my life with the confidence that there's only
one true and living God and His name is Jehovah.
Let me live my life in confidence, not allowing failures and regrets
to overwhelm me but rather choosing wisdom, knowledge, and the
understanding of God as my master keys.

Who but God?

Holds up the heavens above the earth,
keeps the sun, moon, and stars ablaze and afloat,
decorates the earth with an abundance of light,
creates the fishes to swim the oceans, lakes, and rivers,
calls forth the wild beasts to climb the mountains,
roam the woodlands, and sneak out the valleys,
makes the rain to fall upon a thirsty land,
who but God?

Who but God formed man out of the dust of the earth,
gave him the earth as his domain,
placed him in charge of all earthly things,
caused him to multiply and replenish the land,
increased him in wisdom, knowledge, and understanding,
who but God?

Who but God best understands man's going and coming,
his ups and downs?
Who but God best knows and understands his doings?
Who but God can stop the earth from spinning,
the sun, moon, and stars from floating and shining?
Who but God can cause the storms to cease,
bring the all catastrophic acts to an end?
Tell me, who if not God?

Who but God
is in charge of every earthly thing?
Who but God has the final say in man's existence,
destiny, and plans?
Who but God is the authority?
It's time we find out.
It's time we look deep into ourselves.
It's time we observe the seriousness of the time
that we are living in.
It's time we acknowledge that all depends on God.

Who Do We See on Our Streets?

People coming, people going, but who do we see on our streets?
We see the downtrodden, we see the upbeat,
we see the despised, the rejected, the so-called good, and even the bad,
we see the blind, the seeing, and the pitiful.
But with all that we see, we don't seem to see the lost.

We see hungry people waiting to be fed.
We see hurting souls needing to be delivered.
And there are the lost, contrary to what you may believe,
they are never hard to find.
We see them walk across the streets and hop into bars.
We see them entering the nightclubs as the doors sling and open wide.
But with all that we see, do we see them with a compassionate heart?

We see them in the daytime, we see them at nights,
we see them in the darkness, we see them trying to evade the light.
Children and young children lost in the system,
rejected by their parents, defined by their looks and actions

We blame everybody else but never ourselves.
We see where they are going but not where they are coming from.
We criticize their nakedness but never think of clothing them.
We talk about their music but secretly we accept and learn their lyrics.

Oh yes, we see them, everyone.
We see them every day.
We see them marching down to hell but we refuse to help
them to get on the heavenly way.

Why Boast?

Why boast about yourself, you are only mortal?
Why boast as if you hold the world in your hand?
Why boast as if you are the master of everything?
Why boast when knowingly you have only limited control over things?
Why do you find it necessary to look and act as if you are God?
When will you accept that we should only boast in God?

You boast of your wealth.
You boast of your fame.
But why boast as if you can add one measure of stature to your life?
Why boast when you are merely flesh and blood?
You give God no credit for any part played in your life.
You exalt and praise yourself on everything.
You never cease to boast yourself on carnal things.

But where were you when the earth was framed?
Where were you when He spoke things into being?
Where were you in the creation plan?
Where are you as He gives us advice, reminders, and warnings?
Where are you as He daily walks this land?

When will you stop to recognize Him?
When will you acknowledge the power He has?
When will you stop boasting about self
and accept that the Lord alone is God?
When will you accept that you are only mortal man?

Why Do You Wait?

What is it that hinders you, what is it that matters?
What is it that holds you back and keeps you far from others?
What is it that you fail to do to find in Him a friendship that is sweet?
Why do you wait and why do you refuse a better life with Him?
The world with all its beauty and dreams will pass you by.

An invitation He has freely extended.
His arms He holds out wide.
His eyes He keeps steadfast on you all the time.
He gently whispers in your ears,
"What is it for which you wait? Give me your heart, my child."

Will You Fight Back?

Will you just sit back while the devil makes his attacks
or will you fight back with what you have got?
Will you allow yourself to be beaten to a pulp
or will you rise up and take the enemy down and out and off your
track?
It's time to find out how you would react.

I will fight back when I am attacked.
I will fight back and I will not hold back.
I will fight back to send my attacker a message.
I will fight back using the most powerful weapon,
the weapon of love.

I will fight back and I know I will triumph.
I will fight back taking nothing for granted.
I will fight back applying supernatural power.
I must be prepared to fight and win battles for Jesus Christ.
I must always be ready to stand up for the right.
I will fight back using Bible instructions.

Wounded and Left to Die

Broken, wounded, battered, and bruised,
Left in the dark to bleed and die.
Injured, disrobed, hopeless, cut to the throat,
it is ugly and bitter and I am out in the cold.
Calling for help but my cries go unheard,
dear God, what must I do?
A dagger in my heart, an arrow in my back,
and blood oozing out of my side,
bleeding all over, staining every spot,
blood running down all over the ground.

Ruined and wounded and left half dead,
Cursed, abused, and accused by the world,
Maybe that's the life I chose.
Dear God in heaven, hear me now.
I called out for help as the priest passed by,
but he had no time for the destitute such as I.
I called out again as the Levite came by,
he too was busy so he hastened his steps and kept his head high.

They might have heard my groans and cries, but all that they did
was quicken their steps and walked on the other side.
However, I cried out again and again as I felt the growing pains.
I prayed that someone would stop and rescue me,
for deep in my heart I felt I was not going to make it to tell the tale.
Bloodied, weak, wounded, and left to die,
I cried out in desperation to the Lord Jesus Christ.

I felt like I was on the edge of a cliff, ready to fall over into hell's pit.
I did not hear the footsteps of the next person as he drew near.
I was too wounded and filled with pain to hear
or recognize that he was near.
It was a Samaritan who picked me up.
He attended to my wounds from my head to my toes.
He did all he could to preserve my life.
He did all he could to give me a new lease on life.

A miraculous touch was what I got.
The warmth of his presence the touch of his blessed hands
restored and healed my wounded, ruined head, heart, soul, and hands.
Thank God today I live to sing a new and wonderful song.
Thank God for those Samaritans who may come your way
to lend a helping hand to a wounded Jew,
Gentile, or just another human.

You Are Invited, Please Come

You are invited to a grand and glorious feast
planned to take place at the great banquet inn hall.
Come as you are.
Come with an appetite.
Come for a good, healthy, and satisfying meal.
Come ready and prepare to eat all you can eat.

No reservation will be needed.
No formality. In fact, even jeans are accepted.
Seated at the head of the table will be Jesus Christ Himself,
with angels entertaining throughout and around the clock.

There will be room enough for you and all who come.
There will be food just right and ready for your total
consumption and perfect appetite.
Food in abundance, food for all people,
food for all nation, culture, ages, and creed.
For this will be the greatest feast that will ever be
and as advertised. It's all you can drink and eat.

First on the menu will be the salvation dish.
You may eat as much as you wish from it.
The fruit of the Spirit will be served as the dessert,
for you will never be able to function without it.
And now for some added information
and what is most exciting about this,
your entire full course of savory and mouthwatering meal
will be absolutely free and will be to your perfect satisfaction.
And the Host has publicly promised that
there will never be a feast to match this.

All are invited.
All will be united.
All will be treated with the living bread
and the new and finest of wine.
Sign up now, it will be worth it. It will be wonderful
being on the Lord's royal guest list.

You Are Not an Accident

You are not an accident.
You are not a mistake.
For a purpose, you were born.
You are not created to be worthless.
You are designed for something unique, smart, and special.
Even without some vital organs,
you are God's ideal creation.

In God's eye, you are wonderfully made.
If He sees it fit to give you life,
surely it's His absolute right.
Even if He did not choose to give you seeing eyes,
even if He did not choose to give you arms or legs,
even if He did not make you as beautiful
as you think He should.
For even without certain organs or limbs,
He has the plans that are designed to match you.

He can change the paradigm of everything.
He made no mistake in doing things.
He knew way ahead of time about everything.
He has a strategy to make things work out well.
Even though imperfect they may look to our naked eyes,
they are perfect in His sight.

God has the unique ability to do extraordinary things.
He creates surprises and wonders with imperfect
and unusual people and things.
He is creative and marvelous in all His workings.
So quit worrying, you are not an accident.
God can do anything with you.

So let's be still and know that He is a creator and healer.
Let's watch and see Him create wonders.
To see him work, seize the moment now and
call him out,
for He is not sloppy or limited in His works.
Neither is He risky in his behavior.
You are not an accident.
You are in His image, likeness, and His favor.

You Are What You Think and Confess to Be

You are as young as you feel you are.
You are as youthful as you strive to be.
You are as strong as you see in yourself,
Rich as you imagine and think,
Healthy as you add, intake, and output in your body.

Deep down in the heart, in the depth of your being,
and the consciousness of your soul,
you have established a covenant with yourself.
The reality is you are what you believe and confess that you are.
If the message you allow yourself to receive
is optimistic and bright, then it will turn on the light
and cause you to live.
But if the news is fear and despair, you could begin
to shrivel and shake,
lose the will to resist, wallow in imaginary pain,
and die quickly.

Reject going through the pain or stuck in regret,
brighten every path, expecting only the best.
Life is a song and a dance, only those who
know the lyrics and keep practicing the steps
will successfully pass.
So don't worry yourself about the years,
they are only numbers.
There are those who worry to tears.
Numbers are for counting, and as long as nobody
recite them, they'll remain silent on the page.

You Can Be Helped

If you want to encounter God, follow the Bible track.
If you want to walk in the light, contact Jesus Christ
for He is the light.
If you are dealing with darkness
and want to see your way out,
call upon Him, He is the light of the world.
If you desire a better life, get to know Jesus Christ.
He is the Life. He gives Himself away.
If you are looking for the truth, now it's time to act.
Get on the right track,
for only Jesus Christ is the Light, the Life,
the Truth, and the Way.

You Can Live

Plead the blood of Jesus over your life.
The blood of Jesus has power over you.
You can live and not die.
Plead the blood, the blood of Jesus.

Plead the blood of Jesus over your decisions.
Plead it over every aspect of your life.
The blood of Jesus has power to heal
and it is always available to you.

Plead the blood, the blood of Jesus.
Plead the Blood in everything you do.
To defeat death, plead the blood
and watch and see what God will do.

You Can Make a Difference

You can change the world around you.
You can make a significant difference if you choose.
You can affect lives and greatly influence people
because it's in you to make a difference.

God has empowered you to change some things
if you'll listen and trust Him.
You are not here to occupy space
Or just to show your lovely face,
but you are here to demonstrate His love, favor, and grace.
You are here to make a difference,
a difference in the lives of humans.

You can make a difference by your actions and words.
You can make a significant difference
if you'll only take God at His word.
You can make that difference
if you are willing and obedient.
You can make a difference if you only
would follow and trust Him.

You can make a difference living on this land.
You can make a difference if you follow
His divine directions and plans.
You can make a difference beginning now,
O yes, you can.
You can make that difference if you
only submit to Him.

You Can Recover All

You can survive.
You are not bound to circumstances.
You can triumph over adversities.
You can overcome.
You can recover all.

You have been robbed.
You have been beaten down.
Many things that you've been through
are meant to harm, frustrate, weary,
and disarm you, but you can survive.
You don't have to accept or consider
yourself a victim.
That is the devil's lie.

You can recover all.
Stand firm, steadfast, and well,
grounded in the recovery zone.
God's words remain true.
You can survive.
You can overtake.
You can conquer.
You can recover all.

You Don't Know My Story, You Don't Know My Pain

(The Cry of a Deserted Woman)

I write
to make a statement.
I write to say a few words.
I am writing just to let you know
that I know
you don't know what I'm going through.
You don't know my pain.

You don't know my pain.
You see me when I smile,
but, in fact, you don't see me when I shed the tears.
You see me when I seemed full,
but you don't seem to notice what I eat to keep myself alive
and drive away the hunger pain.
You don't know that I don't sleep at nights
but I stay up to plan where my next meal could come from.
You don't seem to see the loneliness in my eyes,
but they exist for I am stressed out, lonely, and in pain.

You don't know what I'm going through.
You don't even seem to care.
All that you know is the color of my skin,
The rags I wear, and
The shame I bear.
You don't know I am your sister. We share the same Father.
You don't even know the first letter of my name.
You don't even know I'm human.
You don't even know that red blood runs through my veins.
You don't even know that sometimes I am forced
to eat from a garbage pile or I'll starve and die.
You don't know my story.
You don't know my pain.

You know nothing about me.
My bruised lips, you do not see,
nor my chained, tired hands and feet.
You may not even have noticed
I lived and walk the streets.
You don't know what I am going through.
You don't know my story.
You don't know my pain.

You Can't Hide from God

There is no place to hide from God's roaming eyes.
Not for a split second, not for a moment in time.
His eyes are sharp, tracking you at all times.
You can't hide from Him.
He has superior twenty-twenty vision.

You may try to dodge from Him,
You may even try the game of hide and seek,
But He is always watching.
Indeed, He doesn't sleep.
You can't hide from Him no matter how hard you try.

You can't hide from Him.
His eyes follow you everywhere,
yet we sometimes wish or think that if we should blink
or wink so we could get away from Him.

He is never weary.
He never naps, slumbers, or sleeps.
He never takes His eyes off you.
He diligently watches over His sheep.

You can't hide from God no matter what you do.
His eyes are always planted on you.
You can't hide from Him no matter how hard you try
Because His eyes are permanently glued on you.

You Claim You Are In Love with Jesus?

You say you are in love with Him,
Yet you stand afar while others defame Him.
You give no allegiance to Him.
You say you are in love with Him,
yet you are not seen walking with Him.
You never talk about Him.
You show no real affection for Him.
You say you are in love with Jesus,
yet you do not know the facts about Him.

You Have an Appointment

An appointment you dare not break.
You have an appointment you cannot change the date.
It's an appointment you have to keep.
An appointment you cannot escape.

You have an appointment that will be fulfilled
at the time appointed.
You cannot run or hide from it.
You have to stick with it, whether you like it or not.
One day you'll meet it face-to-face.
It's an appointment that comes without a given time or date.

With each breath you take, you come closer to it.
And sometimes it will appear as if it is steering you in the face.
It's not a mistake that you have this appointment.
It is authorized.
It's destined.
It's an appointment that has its rights.

As you approach your secret but set date,
live right.
Live your life for Jesus Christ.
Live that when ushered out you'll be ushered into
paradise, God's eternal place, to fulfill your appointment and
mandate.

You Knew

You saw me hungry, but you gave me no food.
You saw me falling, yet you made no attempt to save me.
You saw me wallowing in the mud, you never try to pull me out.
You saw me lying by the roadside, you quickly walked on the other side.
You knew I was a transgressor, yet you did not offer me correction. Instead, you criticized and kept away from me.
You knew that I was homeless, you never offered me a place to rest.
You knew that I had problems, you never offered to help to solve them.
You knew I was drifting away from God, you never try to steer me back to Him.
You never invite me to your church although you knew I was not attending one.
You never offer me help although you knew I was needy and lacking.
You never introduce or mention the name of Jesus to me although you knew I did not know the man.

You May Be Running Out of Time

You have a date that must be kept.
You have a date that is fixed,
a date that is very important in your life.
But are you concerned about it?
Or do you choose to count it like any other date?
Or are you too busy to think about it at this time of your life?

Is everything about you in its rightful place?
Do you have earthly obligations yet to be fulfilled?
Or are you satisfied with the way you think and live?
Are you ready and waiting to meet with the King of kings?
You may be running out of time.

You could be running out of time waiting
on so-called important matters.
You could be running out of time doing
unnecessary things for yourself and others.
The hands of the clock is surely moving fast.
It's important to warn you that time will not last.
So refrain from idle works and deeds,
you have a date, indeed.

There is no time to spare.
Do the right thing, do it now,
or be prepared to see time run out on you.
Waste no more time pursuing things that will not last.
Check the time, you have a date with death.
If you are not ready for it, I can only hope
and pray that your call won't be today.

You Must Be Born Again

Jesus said to the rich young ruler,
"You must be born again."
He's saying it to you, too.
Can you hear Him?
"You must be born again."

You will not have to reenter into
your mother's womb
But you must be born again.
It is a spiritual birth and a miracle that only God can do.
There is no getting around it,
you must be born again.

This is a fact.
This is the truth.
There is no other option.
There is no way.
Take it or leave it.
You must be born again.
This is what Jesus is saying to you.

You must be born again.
To earn yourself eternal life,
that's the requirement.
You must go through the process of transformation,
the regeneration, and the renewing of your mind.
You must have Jesus Christ,
otherwise you will not be qualified.
You must be born again

You've Got to Know My God

The God that rules and reigns in righteousness.
The God of love, joy, peace, and happiness.
The God of truth and mercy.
The God of Abraham, Jacob, and Isaac.
The God of all good thing.

You've got to know my God, the lover and savior of my soul.
The God who conquers death and cause man's soul to rest.
You got to know my God, the God who saves from destruction.
The God of righteous judgment.

You've got to know my God.
The one who anoints with fresh oil and cause man to
flourish like a palm tree and to grow like the cedar of Lebanon.
The God of good plans.
The God who holds man's destiny in His hands.

You've got to know my God.
The God of a second chance.
The God who forgives sins.
The God that offers abundant life
to whosoever that truly ask.

Beverley Bennett—Meet the retired teacher, self-styled playwright, director, poet, passionate reader, advocate of the Word of God, a keen observer of biblical truths, and a person with an ear for rhythm. A woman who writes only in accordance to the script God has given her. A woman that sleeps with a pen and a notepad at her bedside in preparation for the next word from God, a dedicated woman, a committed and unwavering soul.

It's no wonder that God chose her to be His voice, utilizing her passion to bring His message of love, peace, joy, warning, and insights to all who will read this book.

You are invited to join her on this amazing journey and experience into *Dearly Beloved—Apple of God's Eye.*